The Future of the Countryside

ISSUES FOR THE NINETIES

Volume 1

Editor

Craig Donnellan

Independence
Educational Publishers
Cambridge

First published by Independence
PO Box 295
Cambridge CB1 3XP

British Library Cataloguing in Publication Data
The Future of the Countryside – (Issues for the Nineties Series)
I. Donnellan, Craig II. Series
333.7'3'16

ISBN 1 86168 030 9

Printed in Great Britain
City Print Ltd,
Milton Keynes

Typeset by
Claire Boyd

Cover
The illustration on the front cover is by
Michaela Bloomfield.

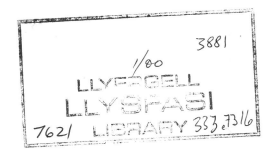

CONTENTS

Introduction

The Future of the Countryside is the first volume in the series: **Issues For The Nineties**. The aim of this series is to offer up-to-date information about important issues in our world.

The Future of the Countryside looks at the changing nature of the countryside as more people choose to live, work and holiday in rural areas. The book also looks at urban improvements as a way of reducing the exodus from cities.

The information comes from a wide variety of sources and includes:
Government reports and statistics
Newspaper reports and features
Magazine articles and surveys
Literature from lobby groups
and charitable organisations.

It is hoped that, as you read about the many aspects of the issues explored in this book, you will critically evaluate the information presented. It is important that you decide whether you are being presented with facts or opinions. Does the writer give a biased or an unbiased report? If an opinion is being expressed, do you agree with the writer?

The Future of the Countryside offers a useful starting-point for those who need convenient access to information about the many issues involved. However, it is only a starting-point. At the back of the book is a list of organisations which you may want to contact for further information.

*****

Love affair with the countryside

Poll probes people's perceptions

Knowing what your customers want is sound business practice, so when the Countryside Commission began preparing a new strategy for the next decade, a first task was to get a better understanding of what people want from England's countryside, and what they value about it. Peter Ashcroft looks at the fascinating findings uncovered in a study and considers their implications

More than nine out of ten people in all walks of life value the English countryside. The sense of relaxation and well-being they get out of enjoying the countryside is all-important, and being able to 'get away from it all' makes a real contribution to people's quality of life.

A rich seam of interest and affection for England's rural heritage emerged from a poll organised by the Countryside Commission, and the findings will inform the development of countryside policies into the next century.

We commissioned a study of public attitudes to the countryside to find out what contribution it makes to people's quality of life. We know the countryside gives personal benefits; we needed to know what they are and what people want the countryside to provide for them in the future.

> *Ninety per cent of people agreed that society has a moral duty to protect the countryside*

We found little existing relevant research, so we held discussions with selected groups, and then carried out a full-scale opinion poll of more than 1,000 adults.

The study unearthed some real revelations and posed some tricky dilemmas. Most of all, it struck a chord of affection for the countryside; our researchers said they had rarely experienced such enthusiasm on the doorsteps of Britain.

For a start, most people considered that farming and caring for the countryside go hand in hand; seven out of ten people believe that farming and forestry keep the countryside an attractive place.

But how important is the countryside in society today? The study showed that environmental issues, including the future of the countryside, come close behind people's main worries about modern life, such as crime, unemployment, traffic and the economy. One in three people expressed great concern about the quality of the countryside.

Strong views

The study explored attitudes to a range of conservation and recreation matters by asking for people's reactions to a number of statements.

Ninety per cent of people agreed that society has a moral duty to protect the countryside for the future and nearly the same number agreed that the countryside should be protected at all costs. Many people accepted that they would have to pay more to protect the countryside in future; they felt that government effort ought to be stepped up, too.

A hidden army of supporters was also detected, with more than four out of ten people saying that they were very keen to get involved in protecting the countryside. This is about ten times the number who currently do get involved in practical conservation work, something of a challenge to all countryside organisations wanting to boost their public support.

There was a very strong desire for greater opportunities for access to the countryside, especially close to where people live: six out of seven people said that more natural open space is needed in and around cities and towns. Three-quarters also felt that there should be more places open to the public next to rivers, lakes, ponds and canals.

While accepting that people sometimes need a reason – an attraction or place of interest – to visit the countryside, seven in ten felt that large-scale leisure facilities are likely to spoil the rural scene.

Six out of ten also expressed a view of the countryside as 'our land' and believed that people should have free access to it. The majority would like more information about where to go and what to see and do.

Personal benefits

We have always known that people gain personal benefits from the countryside; just what these are has been less clear.

By visiting the countryside, people gain a wide range of benefits, both physical and spiritual. The single most important is a sense of relaxation and well-being, which was identified by nearly half of those questioned. A quarter also mentioned fresh air, and more than one in five appreciated the peace and quiet of the countryside. Other benefits included fitness and good health and the chance to 're-charge

A place for work and a need for jobs

There was a sense of realism about the need for economic prosperity and development in rural areas. Virtually no one wanted to see the countryside turned into a museum, and three-quarters recognised it has to be a place where people can make a living.

Sixty per cent of people felt that new buildings should be allowed, as long as good care was taken with the design and choice of materials. Only one in ten people refused to accept the case for new building.

batteries'. The opportunity of seeing wildlife or spending time with family or friends was less important, and only four per cent mentioned solitude as a benefit.

The study also demonstrated the extent to which people benefit from the countryside, 'just knowing it is there', even if they have little or no physical contact with it. Ninety-three per cent personally value the countryside, regardless of whether they visit it or not; this figure varied little between those who live in the countryside and those from inner cities. Nine out of ten also agreed that the countryside is an important part of the nation's heritage. Interestingly, the study showed that many more people have the countryside on their mind than actually live there or visit it; it may be out of sight but not out of mind.

Living up to expectations?

People were asked to judge how well the countryside provided the things they wanted from it. This is difficult to measure. Generally, people are happy with its intrinsic qualities; about half of the people gave a 'good' rating on freedom and relaxation and peace and quiet. About one in three also gave a 'good' rating for physical features, such as trees, views and open spaces.

It scored less well on the provision of specific facilities, such as local places to play or sit. Only one respondent in ten rated the countryside as 'good' for signposted walks and bridleways. This suggests that the countryside is not providing the quality and range of facilities which people expect, but they are prepared to put up with this because their wider desires are being met.

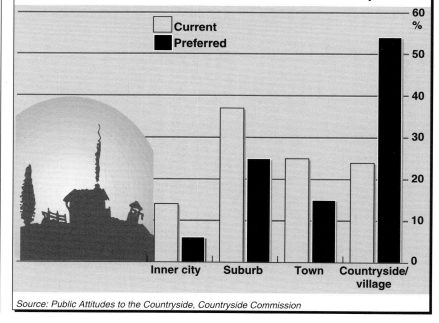

Current versus preferred place of residence

A recent study, *Public Attitudes to the Countryside*, explored what people feel about where they currenly live and where they would ideally like to live. The study found that over half the population prefer to live in the countryside, twice as many as currently do. This implies that there is a substantial market for new homes in the countryside.

Current
Preferred

Inner city   Suburb   Town   Countryside/village

Source: Public Attitudes to the Countryside, Countryside Commission

Worries and concerns

People welcomed the greater level of public awareness of the countryside that exists today, although many were pessimistic for the future. Seventy per cent had seen the countryside change a lot in the last 20 years, and twice as many people named examples of change for the worse as cited changes for the better.

People were concerned about building and over-development, pollution, clearance of hedges and trees, higher volumes of traffic and greater numbers of visitors. There was also a feeling among half of those interviewed that they were just observers, able to see change taking place, but unable to influence it for the better.

What do people want?

People were also asked what they wanted from the countryside in the future. Top of a list of 30 items was local natural open space: two-thirds expressed a need for this. A close second was peace and quiet. More than half also considered unspoiled coasts, woodland, opportunities for seeing wildlife and safe places for children to play as important.

Who are the strongest supporters?

As in most opinion surveys, attitudes varied across the country. Differing shades of opinion were apparent with, for example, stronger feelings about the countryside coming from people living in the south, women rather than men, people with children, those over 30 years of age, those living in the countryside or from higher social groups.

However, these differences were not enough to suggest that the countryside is the concern only of the middle classes. Far from it. Concerns for the countryside exist across the social spectrum, in a way rarely seen in opinion polls.

What this means for the countryside

The study confirms just how important the countryside is to people from all walks of life. It has uncovered a deep-seated attachment to the country-side and revealed many strongly-held beliefs about how it

should be dealt with in the future. So what does this mean for the countryside?

The following conclusions are immediately apparent:

Local is beautiful

People value the countryside, especially near where they live. They strongly support the idea of having more open spaces in and around towns and cities, and having the means to get there without having to use cars. This means that action on people's doorsteps would reap the greatest benefits and be appreciated by the majority.

Public support still untapped

The countryside clearly matters to many millions of people, and not just country dwellers or frequent visitors. There is still a larger constituency of support for its conservation than has so far been tapped; countryside organisations, environmental groups, local and national politicians, take note.

Demand for new homes

Many people aspire to live in the countryside and most are prepared to accept the inevitable growth in new homes and other developments. Even if real demand is only a fraction of that shown by the study, it does

reinforce claims by planners and developers that there is a substantial market for new rural homes. We need to ensure that all new building is of high quality, of good design and in keeping with local character.

Green leisure

People want a better choice of places to visit in the countryside, but they don't want leisure to be a negative force. Despite the sophistication, thrills and choice of today's leisure opportunities, they still seek the relatively simple pleasure that comes from contact with the countryside. People want a welcoming, but not a fossilised, countryside, and there is a continuing need to improve their enjoyment, in terms of quality and variety and in ways that involve less dependence on the car.

The complete study will make fascinating reading for politicians, planners, countryside staff, farmers and landowners, and it offers vital market intelligence for all with responsibilities for England's countryside.

● The above is a summary of a report, *Public attitudes to the country-side*, published by the Countryside Commission. See page 39 for address details.　　　　©*Countryside January/February 1997*

Royal Commission adds to fears over Britain's vanishing fields

By Charles Clover, Environment Editor

The urban area of Britain is likely to double in the next 100 years, with south-east England losing what remains of its rural character, a Royal Commission will report later this month.

The Royal Commission on Environmental Pollution will add its voice to anxieties about the loss of rural land aroused by official research.

Figures show that the equivalent of 27 new towns the size of Milton Keynes will be necessary to meet housing needs in the next two decades. The commission will warn that almost a fifth of England could have disappeared under houses, buildings and roads by the end of the next century to satisfy population growth and the shrinking of the family into small units.

This would be a dramatic increase in urbanisation from just over a tenth of the land area today.

'There will be a substantial difference to our landscape,' said one commission member.

One of the commission's main recommendations will be that housing on the best-quality rural land should be tightly controlled to maintain food production in the next century, when the world population is expected to double to more than 10 billion.

'We are looking at England's green and pleasant land, what it's going to be like in 100 years' time, and what we are going to do about it,' said the source.

'We are going to lose agricultural and green field sites. We must ask if we wish to do that. 'We will also consider the amenity value and biodiversity value of land – which many people feel very strongly about.'

If people are going to build on contaminated plots, then the land must be cleaned up at a faster rate, said the source.

The commission is noted for taking a long-term view on key issues – its last monumental report was on transport, which recommended that petrol taxes should double and that the road-building programme should be halved. Its latest report looks at Britain's soil and calls for the preservation of fertile agricultural land to be given a higher priority within the planning system, as it was in the 'dig for victory' wartime era.

> **Figures show that the equivalent of 27 new towns the size of Milton Keynes will be necessary to meet housing needs in the next two decades**

The commission will recommend the 'best practicable environmental option' for accommodating some of the development that is predicted over the next few years within the planning system.

It has also considered the optimum density of housing schemes and whether wildlife or agricultural productivity is greatly affected if farmland becomes gardens.

Commission members were surprised to discover how many thousands of tons of industrial and food waste were ploughed into the land as soil treatment each year.

The commission will recommend that more waste should be reduced at source or recycled and not used as landfill.

Its report will also criticise the practice of removing contaminated land and dumping it elsewhere. Instead, the commission intends to recommend that pollution-eating bacteria should be used more often to clean land on site, as has been done in other countries.

Further criticism of the Government's present policy of freeing land to meet housing 'need', set out in its household projections, is expected this spring.

It will come from the Commons Environment Committee, which is concluding its inquiry into housing.

City exodus threat to rural areas

By Clare Longrigg

Families escaping the noise and pollution of the city are consuming the countryside and destroying the heart of its towns, says a report by an urban regeneration campaigner.

As rural areas, small market towns and villages are rapidly devoured by the suburban sprawl, town centres are emptying and urban communities vanishing.

A report to be published this week by the Civic Trust, an independent environmental charity, says cities are losing their vitality and urban communities are draining away.

Big cities such as Manchester and Glasgow have lost up to a third of their population in the past 30 years as families seek fresh air and green fields. In Glasgow the population has shrunk from more than a million in 1960 to 623,000. Liverpool has shrunk by 39 per cent since the 1960s. Even older, attractive towns such as York and Chester are being abandoned for the countryside.

'This sort of development doesn't help the towns or the countryside,' said Mike Gwilliam, director of the Civic Trust. 'We are concerned with trying to make cities and towns better, to encourage people to stay in towns and come back . . . We need more emphasis on urban regeneration to make cities more attractive.'

In what Mr Gwilliam describes as our 'anti-city culture', housing in cities is critically under-funded. It often costs more to redevelop derelict sites than to build from scratch. At the same time swathes of rural Britain are being developed within commuting distance of cities.

These stretch across green belt. The biggest cuts across Cambridgeshire, through Buckinghamshire to Newbury, in Berkshire, and Southampton. Other sites are eating up green fields from Manchester, through Birmingham, and from North Wales through to Cardiff and Bristol.

Big cities such as Manchester and Glasgow have lost up to a third of their population in the past 30 years as families seek fresh air and green fields

Steven Norris, the former transport minister and MP for Epping Forest, is backing environment protesters in opposing new roads and claims Britain should stop trying to 'pander to infinite traffic growth'.

Mr Norris's U-turn on Government transport policy comes in an interview with the BBC1 programme Panorama . He also claims the wrong route was chosen for the Newbury bypass.

Shrinkage

- Population of Glasgow has shrunk from more than 1 million in 1960 to 623,000 today

- Population of Liverpool has declined from 750,000 to just under 500,000 in the same period

- Manchester has lost up to a third of its population in 30 years

- Population of rural areas will increase by 30 per cent by 2001

- DoE figures show steady decline in spending on urban regeneration. © *The Guardian March, 1997*

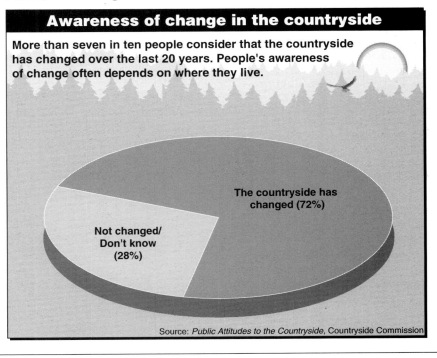

Awareness of change in the countryside

More than seven in ten people consider that the countryside has changed over the last 20 years. People's awareness of change often depends on where they live.

The countryside has changed (72%)

Not changed/ Don't know (28%)

Source: *Public Attitudes to the Countryside*, Countryside Commission

British still seek a rural idyll, and ruin it

Annually, 100,000 people move out of Britain's cities, turning the very countryside they seek into soulless suburbia. Robin McKie reports

Every day, 300 people abandon city life in Britain. Car exhausts, fouled pavements, asthma, fear of crime, traffic jams and poor housing all combine to make urban life intolerable.

This exodus represents an annual outflow of 100,000 individuals, an emigration of the disaffected that has gone on for decades. Millions have decamped from UK cities since World War II.

The basic cause goes beyond simple urban deprivation. That is only a symptom. The real malaise is rooted in British culture, say geographers and planners.

In Western Europe, most citizens have learned how to come to terms with life in conurbations. For example, Parisians, Milanese and Berliners display an enjoyment of café society and promenading that contrasts with Britons' sullen hostility to their own cities. We neglect them, let them decay, and hate them even more as a result.

Instead, the British are obsessed with seeking out a rural idyll – in numbers that are turning precious vestiges of the countryside into soulless suburban enclaves. Berkshire, split by the M4, is almost an entire dormitory county today, and Hampshire, cleft by the M3, faces a similar fate.

In one survey, 81 per cent of respondents said they would prefer to have their home in a village or small English town. Yet more than 70 per cent of the UK population actually lives in a city, despite recent exoduses. 'Most of our population dwell in cities but have their hearts in the country,' said Geoff Mulgan of the think-tank Demos.

Inexorably, these country-lovers are seeping out of cities and peppering the landscape with motorways, business parks, out-of-town hypermarkets and fringe housing estates. Every year, an area of countryside the size of Bristol is built over in the process.

> ### In one survey, 81 per cent of respondents said they would prefer to have their home in a village or small English town

'People are obliterating the very things they desire,' said Tony Burton of the Council for the Protection of Rural England (CPRE). 'At the same time, cities are increasingly being left to dereliction.'

And there is no sign of the rot stopping. Environment Secretary John Gummer recently announced that of the 4.4 million new homes to be built in Britain over the next 20 years, half are to be erected outside cities, despite the lethal pressures that already afflict rural land and the neglect of inner-city sites.

In other words, Britain's urban antipathy is now irrevocably damaging our entire landscape, a trend that so alarms planners and geographers that they are pressing for major investment programmes and tight rural planning restrictions to halt the destruction.

'These measures are crucially needed, though we also have to understand why we don't like cities in the first place,' said Charles Landray. In his book, *The Creative City*, he traces much of the country's urban woes to the Industrial Revolution, which occurred first in Britain and had a much more devastating effect than elsewhere. Large tracts of city land were quickly turned into squalid, unhygienic ghettos. On the Continent, develop-ers learnt from our example and created far less desolate landscapes.

Development and economics

People have a sense of realism about development and economic growth in the countryside. The table below shows that most people accept that population growth across England means that towns and cities will expand into the countryside. Many also feel that the countryside has to be a 'living place' where people can work as well as play.

	Total %	Strongly agree %	Slightly agree %
Population growth in this country means that towns and cities will have to expand into the countryside	78	31	47
The countryside has to be a place where people can make a living	76	31	45
New building should be allowed in the countryside as long as good care is taken with design and use of materials	59	16	43

Source: Public Attitudes to the Countryside, Countryside Commission

'Cities became places where you could celebrate some sense of liberation, as you can see in the works of Baudelaire and Manet. Dickens merely depicts them as grim points of exploitation, by contrast,' says Landray.

'And merchants who made their fortunes from steam or steel here merely aped the aristocracy – and built country mansions. Cities were for the poor.' In fact, the division is not so much a European-British one as an English-Continental one. In Scotland, particularly in Glasgow and Edinburgh, where tenement flats provide the dominant form of accommodation, cities are more European in attitude. City-dwellers there have made their pact with their environment, unlike their English counterparts.

'In England, city-dwellers have a great passion for houses and gardens,' said Ken Worpole, of the think-tank Comedia. 'They persist in believing this rural myth and have spent years trying to turn cities into the countryside. Now they are turning the countryside into cities.'

A measure of England's urban antipathy is provided by census analyses carried out by Tony Champion, reader in geography at Newcastle University. These show that the net annual surplus of disaffected urbanites (generally the retired, the self-employed or those sick of commuting) over new city-lovers (usually young adults leaving the country to find work or further education) is around 100,000.

'In 1987, during the boom, it was 125,000 a year. Then in 1990, during the recession, it dropped to 65,000 when the property market collapsed. Now it is back up to 90,000. In other words, the urge to leave cities is as strong as ever. Only economics limits the flow.'

If unchecked, this urge is likely to have an immense impact on the nation. If concrete and tarmac spread at the present rate, an area of countryside the size of Greater London will have been built over by the year 2016. Something, say the planners, must be done.

'The root of the problem lies with the city,' said the CPRE's Burton. 'People are being pushed out, rather than being pulled into the country. We have to make cities more attractive places in which to live.'

Transport forms much of the focus for the attentions of groups such as the CPRE, with cars being pinpointed as the main source of misery for city-dwellers. They induce 'urban immobility' for children. Parents are so fearful their children will be knocked down if they walk or ride a bike that they take them everywhere by car themselves. This loss of freedom induces frustration in children.

Every year,
an area of countryside
the size of Bristol
is built over

In addition, exhaust fumes are linked to spiralling asthma rates in children, and gridlocked roads, particularly London's, send travelling times soaring.

Major investment in city public transport is sought as a priority for protecting the countryside, though other measures are also needed. At present, it is still cheaper to build on virgin land than reclaim old inner-city industrial or housing sites. Tax incentives to help the latter, at the expense of the former, are also urged by groups such as the Civic Trust.

The trust points to the soullessness of many urban areas, which are increasingly monitored by closed-circuit television rather than patrolled by police, and also to the remoteness of decision-making in town and city centres, where local bank and store managers have no autonomy, despite their importance to their community.

But perhaps the most important factor is pride and involvement. 'Restoring that to cities would reap enormous dividends,' said Paul Davies, director of the trust's regeneration unit.

In cities such as Glasgow, which has striven to create a unique cultural identity for itself in recent years, and Manchester, with its vibrant pubs and clubs, there is evidence this can be done. The task is elusive. 'The crucial point is that it can be done,' added Davies.

© The Observer
May, 1996

Townies 'to blame for crisis in the country'

Council leaders are planting traffic pollution 'timebombs' in the countryside, the Government claimed yesterday. They help create a demand for new roads by encouraging the spread of out-of-town shopping centres and business parks, said Planning Minister Robert Jones. The Government wanted businesses to stay in city centres, but it was difficult to get the message across to 400 planning authorities, who often put jobs before the environment, said Mr Jones. He was replying to a report by a group of businessmen warning against over-development on 'green' sites.

A place in the country, with the village pub and shop just by the green, used to be what dreams were made of.

But now all that is being ruined by the very people who moved house in search of the rural idyll, it was claimed yesterday.

City slickers with sleek cars and mobile phones are turning once thriving villages into virtual dormitories for large towns.

Instead of supporting village life, they shop in superstores – leading to pubs, shops and bus routes closing through lack of business, said Richard Wakeford, chief executive of the Countryside Commission.

'People are spending money in superstores while bemoaning the loss of traditional greengrocers and butchers' shops,' Mr Wakeford told the Royal Town Planning Institute. 'They then criticise the loss of rural bus services they have never used.'

He warned that new choices in transport, schools, shopping, work and leisure were transforming the old ways.

The village crisis had worsened recently as families spill out of towns and cities upsetting traditional patterns of life – and locals who have lived there all their lives.

Estimates suggest 4.4 million new homes will be needed over the next 20 years to meet demand.

Suzanne Walker, of the Campaign for the Protection of Rural England, lives in Thaxted, Essex, where the population has swelled by almost a third to 2,500 in the last 25 years.

A place in the country, with the village pub and shop just by the green, used to be what dreams were made of

---

'There has been a great increase in houses but a massive decline in services,' she said. 'It has to be said that because people don't use them, that is why we are losing them.'

Ian Brodie, of the Friends of the Lake District, admitted there was often tension in an area popular for holiday and retirement homes.

'Many rural areas suffer from conflict between old communities and new members who often don't understand what they are moving into,' he said.

'They forget the countryside is a noisy place where cocks crow, cows moo and pigs oink. They say the streets are dark and they want lighting. Then they want a road across the village green so they can get to their houses easier.

'But new people often have skills that can be put to good use in preserving village life. If they can integrate, they have a role to play.'

© The Daily Mail
February, 1997

£1m shopping offer that divides a town

By Chris Brooke

One subject unites the people of Settle in agreement – their need for a new primary school.

The prospect of a supermarket in the North Yorkshire market town has entirely the opposite effect.

But in the manner of modern planning battles, the two possibilities have become entwined.

A £1 million school is the sweetener offered by one of several store groups bidding for permission to build in Settle.

It comes from Preston-based supermarket chain Booths. Three rival proposals are also under consideration.

As planners from Craven District Council prepare to make the final decision, the arguments have raged.

One side, led by the town's traders and traditionalists, believe the school scheme is 'immoral'. They also insist that Settle, with a population of 2,340, is too small for a supermarket.

Others argue that a new store would benefit the consumer and a new school would help the community.

County councillor Beth Graham said: 'The town is certainly divided by this. Some people have been getting exceedingly heated about the whole issue. I'm glad I am not on the planning committee.' The town's current Church of England school has 142 pupils, with 30 in the nursery. It is cramped and said to be in 'desperate need' of replacement, but no money is available.

Gerard Glynn, a baker, described the plan to link the supermarket approval to a new school as 'immoral and appalling'.

He added: 'Our population is so small there are more sheep than people around here.

'Nobody would argue with the fact that we need a new school but we don't need a new superstore.'

Would-be developers will face tough questioning from residents at a public meeting to discuss the plans next week.

Councils 'ignore guideline on out-of-town shopping'

By Charles Clover, Environment Editor

Out-of-town developments that can be reached only by car are getting planning permission three years after the Government said no more should be built, a report said yesterday.

A list of shopping centres, multiplex cinemas, business parks and housing schemes, with permission or still being considered, was published by the Council for the Protection of Rural England.

The council said the deliberate disregard of guidelines was 'creating a future of traffic jams and suburban sprawl which will cost the countryside dearly'.

Councils, and on occasion the Government itself, ignored Planning Policy Guidance note 13, a major turn-around in planning launched in 1994.

This aims to reduce the need to travel, particularly by car, and to protect the vitality of city centres.

One of the largest car-based developments with planning permission is the West Wood holiday village, in 400 acres of Lyminge Forest, Kent. The site, which takes 4,000 visitors, has a traffic-free zone but the only way of reaching it is by car.

Another development is Star Site leisure complex, the biggest cinema complex in Europe, next to the M6 near Spaghetti Junction. The site has 30 screens.

In Newcastle upon Tyne, the city council proposes to make one of the largest-ever releases of green belt land to create a development area, including 2,500 executive homes and a 200-acre business park.

Planning permissions get through because planning guidance is not law. Protest groups have to seek judicial review of a decision on the basis of failure 'adequately to reflect' the weight of planning guidance in making a decision.

Lilli Matson, head of transport at the Council for the Protection of Rural England, said: 'It's crazy, isn't it? Supermarkets caught the sharp end of the planning guidance but housing developments, business parks, leisure developments and cinemas go on getting built.'

How to campaign on supermarket developments

Information from Sustainable Agriculture, Food & Environment (S.A.F.E)

Retail impact: the effect of supermarket development on existing town centres

The effect of a superstore on an existing town centre is referred to as the retail impact. This briefing gives some background information on these effects as well as explaining current Government policy and why this is an important issue for local campaigners. There is also an explanation of retail impact studies and a guide to criticising those studies produced by the supermarket's consultants.

National trends on supermarket expansion

The most recent national figures show that the trend towards fewer, larger stores and edge- and out-of-town supermarkets is continuing. A recent study by the retail consultants Verdict found that the number of superstores will grow by 25 per cent during the next five years.

National policy on retail impact

The Government has set out how local authorities should assess retail proposals, and you can check that your council is doing so. The matters to be taken into account where proposals are outside existing town centres are:

- The impact on the development plan strategy
- The impact on the vitality and viability of existing centres
- Accessibility – new development should be located where a significant proportion of customers and staff will be able to get to the development by means other than car

The likely cumulative effect of recently completed retail developments and outstanding planning permissions should also be taken into account when assessing the impact of a proposal.

Until July 1996 Government advice to local councils was that planning permission for retail development should not be refused on the grounds of retail impact 'unless there was clear evidence to suggest that the result would be to undermine the vitality and viability of a centre, which would otherwise continue to serve the community well'. This put great stress on the assessment of retail impact. The new Planning Policy Guidance 6 (PPG6) will reduce the weight attached to retail impact studies by placing greater emphasis on the overall impact on travel patterns.

Why are town centres important?

Town centres are part of our national and civic heritage. They can provide a focus for civic pride and a sense of place and local identity. They contain many of the public cultural assets like museums, libraries, attractive or distinctive townscape, and public squares and gardens. They play a significant role in the social life of the community as people who visit the centre for a variety of purposes meet and talk in the street. This engenders a sense of belonging to a place and community.

Protecting town centres also promotes sustainable development. They are easily served by public transport, and because many activities are concentrated in the one place, one trip can serve many purposes. Town centres facilitate competition because you can compare prices and goods in different shops easily. In contrast, to buy something expensive from an out-of-town store might involve trips backwards and forwards across town to compare the goods of several such stores.

Town centres are also important because they are accessible to all and not just to those with cars. Nationally about 33.3% of households do not own cars. Many of these people are elderly and find walking long distances and carrying shopping difficult. Many more people, particularly women with young children, cannot use their car during the day, when their husbands are using it to get to work.

The language used in describing the functions and value of town centres is often abstract and can appear to have little to do with your experience. This is because 'experts' find it as difficult as you do to explain what goes on in town centres. If you can explain yourself more directly you will be doing everyone a favour.

Many towns grew up as markets at crossroads where the largest number of people could get to. In time, people offering other services and making goods would go there to take advantage of the people already there. Much later, employers who required large workforces would locate in town centres because they could draw on a larger pool of potential labour. These employees would spend money in shops, further strengthening the town centre. This interdependence of activities is the key to the vitality and viability of town centres. Retailing nevertheless continues to underpin the success of town centres – most people go there to shop.

In many smaller market towns, the supermarket has become the main reason why most people go to town centres. Other reasons for visiting have been progressively withdrawn from many centres. Work is now dispersed to peripheral estates, or concentrated in larger towns. Banks are closing smaller branches. Gas and electricity bills are paid direct or by post and Government or local authorities are centralising their offices in larger towns. If trade is withdrawn from the town centre supermarket to a new out-of-town-centre store, other shops will close because they rely for their own trade on people who shop at the supermarket. This can have a 'snowball' effect, leading to further shop closures and undermining the whole social function of the centre.

Taking action

Look for flaws

Is the developer's assessment of expected turnover realistic? How does it compare with similar outlets from the same company elsewhere? What about town centre stores? If turnover is grossly underestimated this would mean lower retail and traffic impacts, and could make the difference as to whether retail impact is considered significant or not.

Convenience shopping

The stated turnover of the store will be the (minimum) amount of trade which will be lost to existing shops. How much of the store's trade will be main shopping and how much 'top-up' or 'convenience' shopping? Most

supermarkets now are going for the top-up shopping sector of the food market, as well as the main weekly shop. If the store will encourage people to do their top-up shopping by car, such as in the case of an edge of centre site with generous free parking, then this is likely to increase the number of car journeys, since this will replace trips previously made by foot to local shops. Sometimes top-up trips represent the largest number of trips to stores.

Comparison shopping

How many people going to supermarkets in the town centre also spend money on comparison goods, e.g. pots and pans? You can get this information either from the retail consultant or from going into comparison goods shop and asking them.

Thin end of the wedge

Is there room to expand on the site? Might the developer decide to build a DIY store next to the supermarket, or to add an extension to their store? Once permission is given for a superstore, it will be difficult to turn down further development on the site. Clues to such future plans might include a car park far in excess of what is needed. How much of the building will be put over to sales area and how much to storage. Is this comparable with other, similar, recently constructed stores of the company? Most supermarkets today

are served by 'just-in-time' deliveries, which means that goods are delivered when they are needed, minimising the area needed for storage? Might the company be considering moving the internal wall to expand the retail floor space?

Town centre supermarkets

How much trade can existing food shops afford to lose without closing? Even large supermarkets may be vulnerable. Point out that if a large store does close, it will be difficult to re-let the building, with an out-of-town supermarket to draw trade away, while the council's approval of an out-of-town development suggests it has little commitment to the existing shopping centre. Is it likely to be used for anything else or will it remain empty, blighting the area and making it a more unpleasant place to shop?

Also, if a major town centre supermarket closes, surrounding shops will lose 'footfall' and suffer too. Non-food shops, such as chemists, newsagents, off-licences, are also likely to lose trade directly from the proposed development. For struggling small shops, even a 15% reduction in trade may be enough to force closure.

• The above is an extract from a leaflet published by Sustainable Agriculture, Food & Environment (S.A.F.E.) See page 39 for address details. *©S.A.F.E Alliance*

Responding to planning applications

The planning system exists to make sure the public interest in the countryside is properly protected when new development is proposed. Many developments require planning permission from the local planning authority for the area, which usually involves submitting a planning application. You are entitled to comment on these applications. This checklist outlines the steps you can take to present your views on planning applications properly and effectively, to the correct people.

How do I make sure that I hear of a planning application of interest to me?

Are you:

- scanning local newspapers which contain lists of the more important applications?
- asking the local planning authority to tell you of applications likely to be of interest to you?
- obtaining a weekly list of planning applications (there may be a charge for this) if you are expecting to take a long-term interest in them?
- checking for a site notice on or by the vulnerable land?
- asking neighbours adjoining vulnerable land and the parish council (where there is one) to tell you if they receive notification of any planning application?

Has work started apparently without planning permission?

- Check with the local planning authority that the work did get permission (some developments do not need publicity and others do not need to obtain planning consent). If it did not get permission when it was needed, ask if the planning authority are taking enforcement action.

COUNCIL FOR THE PROTECTION OF RURAL ENGLAND

What are the likely impacts of the proposal?

Have you:

- examined the planning application and related maps, plans and supporting documents (available for inspection at the planning department of the local authority – and the parish council may have a copy)?
- visited the site of the proposed development and its surroundings to assess the likely effects of the scheme?

Will the proposal affect my interest in the environment? Ask yourself these questions:

- will the proposal enhance the countryside?
- will it damage the countryside or make problems worse?
- what might go wrong on this land in the future if this application is approved?
- is the development really necessary?
- if so, is this the best place for the development?
- are there other, more benign, ways to achieve the same benefits?
- what measures will be necessary to mitigate its bad effects (you can suggest conditions to be attached to any planning consent)?
- do I ignore, support or oppose the application?

- if opposing, would my objections be resolved by imposing suitable conditions on a permission?

Am I making my case most effectively?

- have you examined the policies in the approved plan or plans for the area (the Structure and Local Plans are available in your public library or from the local planning authority or parish council)?
- does the proposal fit or jar with the policies (the planning application will be decided on how it fits with the plan)?
- do the policies support your view?
- have you checked the view of your local CPRE branch (telephone number in phone book or through address below)?
- have you sent your comments in writing to the correct local authority at the correct address within the time allowed?
- have you gathered support for your views from local people, local organisations, councillors, local authority officials, the media and your MP?
- have you asked the planning officer dealing with the case for help if you are puzzled by procedure or planning policy?
- do you need the fuller *Responding to Planning Applications* booklet which can be obtained from CPRE free of charge?
- have you taken advantage of CPRE's other helpful publications and got a free catalogue from the address below?

• CPRE helps people to protect their local countryside from threat. CPRE Publications, 25 Buckingham Palace Road, London SW1W 0PP Tel: 0171-976-6433 Fax: 0171-976-6373
© CPRE
Autumn, 1996

Save our shops with car tax on malls, say MPs

By John Deans, Chief Political Correspondent

A tax should be slapped on car parks at out-of-town shopping and leisure centres, MPs demanded yesterday.

Supermarkets and multiplex cinemas should pay a levy or additional business rates to cover free parking provided for customers, a cross-party group declared.

The recommendation by the Commons Environment Committee came amid concern that shopping malls on 'greenfield' sites will create more ghost towns by taking business from the high streets.

The MPs welcomed government action curbing the growth of out-of-town centres, saying: 'The situation is much improved.'

But with supermarkets now targeting traditional market towns, the committee called on ministers to deter such developments by forcing up parking costs.

Committee chairman Andrew Bennett said: 'The threat to smaller towns is very real and we want assurances that they will be protected.'

Expressing alarm at the pace and scale of new leisure sites, the Labour MP added: 'Most of these appear to be multiplex cinemas with 20 or 30 screens, sometimes with bowling alleys and food outlets.

'They are a threat to town centres as places where people not only shop, but live, work and relax.'

If a car parking levy or extra business rates were imposed, it would be for the owners or operators to cover the cost themselves or pass it on to customers.

The report also recommended a tougher approach by planning authorities, full impact studies to accompany applications for large retail developments, and the reconsideration of approval already given to projects which have still to get off the ground.

It called for tax relief on private funds used for town centre schemes.

© *The Daily Mail*
March, 1997

New homes best sited in towns, says Minister

By Charles Clover, Environment Editor

U sing green-field sites to build all of the 4.4 million new homes needed in the next 20 years would cause 'wholly unacceptable' environmental damage, John Gummer, the Environment Secretary, said yesterday.

Commenting on a discussion paper released by the Government on where to build the new homes, which were needed as a result of population growth, divorce and people living longer, Mr Gummer said towns had to be made 'more attractive places so that people want to live in them'.

He added: 'This means less crime, a high standard of education and decent housing.'

Mr Gummer said he would be canvassing the public on whether a new target of accommodating 60 per

By 2016 about 11.9 per cent of England's land area would be in urban use compared with 10.6 per cent in 1991

cent of the homes on previously-developed land – 10 per cent more than the present government target – would be enough 'or whether we should do even better'.

The figure of 60 per cent was lower than Mr Gummer had been hinting might be possible and was greeted with disappointment by conservationists.

However, the House Builders' Federation described the figure as 'unrealistic' and the Royal Town Planning Institute said it was 'unreasonable' to those who lived in cities to build so many new homes on urban sites. Mr Gummer's new target would still require 1.76 million new homes to be built on green-field sites.

A report published yesterday with the discussion document said the greatest increase in the total number of houses in shire counties would be in Hampshire (more than 160,000) followed by Cambridgeshire, Essex and Kent (more than 120,000 each). The fastest rates of urban growth would be in Cambridgeshire, Somerset and Devon.

By 2016 about 11.9 per cent of England's land area would be in urban use compared with 10.6 per cent in 1991, a change of 12.2 per cent.

Mr Gummer said that projections carried out in the last 10 years had all been underestimates. 'Doing nothing in the face of these figures is not a responsible way of planning for the future,' he said.

'One thing has to be taken as read. This is that we should provide as many as possible of these new units on land which has already been used, particularly that land which is found within our towns and cities.

'If our urban areas are to be successful in attracting people to live there and retaining existing populations, then we need to give serious consideration to the current problems and apparent disadvantages of living in the city.' Mr Gummer's discussion document, *Household Growth: Where Shall We Live?*, seeks public reactions to a variety of options including extensions to existing towns, extensions to selected 'key' villages, multiple village extensions and free-standing new towns and villages.

Mr Gummer is seeking written responses from individuals and public bodies to the questions raised by his report.

But the consultation period ends on March 17, only a few weeks before the last possible date for a general election, so it is uncertain how much Mr Gummer will be able to change.

Just under half of the projected 4.4 million households are to come into being as a result of the increase in the population. The next largest increase (33 per cent) is due to changes in behaviour, such as the increased rate of households being formed as a result of later marriages and more divorces and separations.

Mr Gummer said in his

> *'If our urban areas are to be successful in attracting people . . . we need to give serious consideration to the current problems and apparent disadvantages of living in the city'*

introduction that it was not for him 'to make moral judgements about the choices which underlie these changes'.

'It is however necessary for all of us to face up to the cumulative environmental impact of the way in which we have chosen to live.' The Council for the Protection of Rural England said it was disappointed with the 'modest' target for house building in urban areas.

'A commitment to building at least 60 per cent of new housing on urban land, while welcome, fails to grasp fully the opportunity for urban renewal in which the quality of life for everyone is improved and the

countryside protected,' said Tony Burton, chief planner.

He said the 60 per cent figure would mean that the existing policy for forcing counties to accommodate higher numbers of homes than they were prepared for would continue.

Roger Humber, of the House-builders' Federation, said: 'We are extremely concerned about the unrealistic targets being set for development in urban areas. We believe that to expect an ever-growing percentage of new homes to be built on reclaimed land will deny a quality of housing and environment to those expected to live in the urban areas.'

The Civic Trust welcomed the target, which it said would be 'tough to achieve'. Michael Gwilliam, director, called for a new tax on green-field development to pay for the extra cost of developing in towns.

The Royal Town Planning Institute warned against 'town cramming'. Tony Struthers, senior vice-president, said: 'We must not recreate the mistakes of the 1960s where people were crammed into hastily and badly-developed buildings.' © *Telegraph Group Limited, London 1996*

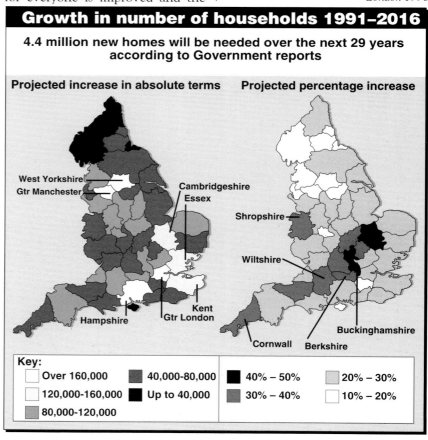

Growth in number of households 1991–2016

4.4 million new homes will be needed over the next 29 years according to Government reports

Projected increase in absolute terms

West Yorkshire
Gtr Manchester
Cambridgeshire
Essex
Hampshire
Kent
Gtr London

Projected percentage increase

Shropshire
Wiltshire
Cornwall
Berkshire
Buckinghamshire

Key:

☐ Over 160,000	■ 40,000-80,000
☐ 120,000-160,000	■ Up to 40,000
▨ 80,000-120,000	

■ 40% – 50%	☐ 20% – 30%
■ 30% – 40%	☐ 10% – 20%

Ghastly sign of the times

Speed restrictions, traffic 'calming' orders, tourist hoardings . . . village residents are furious about the latest rural threat. Caroline McGhie reports

They arrive silently in the night, like creatures from urban space. The residents of Nether Wallop, Middle Wallop and Over Wallop know all about it. One day the villages looked gentle, rural, sleepy. The next day, speed-limit signs sprang up in all directions, and the lanes began to look awkwardly towny.

The Wallops, three Hampshire villages threaded together, are much admired for their beauty. Chalk and flint cottages with tidy thatched roofs sit beside the Wallop brook and weeping willows. The trouble is that a main route between Andover and Salisbury runs through Middle Wallop, along which cars fly at 70 mph.

'Something had to be done about the speed,' said Mrs Margaret Uloth, who lives in Nether Wallop. The village had asked Hampshire County Council for a speed limit along the main road, but then found itself showered with no fewer than 19 signs insisting on 30mph along all the exits and entrances. 'The problem is, they put up these signs everywhere, with repeater signs every 100 yards, sometimes right in front of people's houses.'

There was bewilderment among the villagers. 'The signs were put up in tiny winding lanes where you would crash if you drove at 30mph. They even blocked people's sightlines round corners,' said Mrs Uloth. 'Frankly, villagers have been going out and digging them up and moving them.'

Sadly, the Wallops are not alone. Villages all over the country are having to come to terms with the fact that the volume of traffic funnelling through is predicted to triple in some counties in the next 30 years.

According to an independent study commissioned by the Council for the Protection of Rural England (CPRE), Bedfordshire, Cambridgeshire, Dorset, Nottinghamshire and Sussex are all likely to be badly affected. The English village scene is now seriously threatened by roadside paraphernalia.

> *Villages all over the country are having to come to terms with the fact that the volume of traffic funnelling through is predicted to triple in some counties in the next 30 years*

The changes happen in small stages, each change usually too minor for people to protest about, yet overall the impact is profound and irreversible. Grassy verges are hardened by kerbstones, dark rural skies are turned a sodium orange by street-lamps, gentle lanes are remodelled into urban streets with chicanes and pinchpoints, hedgerows are peppered with speed signs.

Then the petrol companies add their corporate livery to the mix; car-boot sale organisers erect their hand-drawn placards; ice-cream sellers vie for passing trade with museums, fun-factories and historic sites; and soon the prettiest parts of the countryside are plastered with advertising, some of it from the most unexpected quarters.

One morning in April this year, Colin Wales woke up in Appleton Roebuck to find York City gateway signs erected on the rim of the village, some six miles from the city itself. 'They were large, about six-foot by four-foot, and glaring blue. It came as a real shock. Everyone was talking

about them,' he said. The signs said Welcome To The City of York.

His investigations revealed that York City Council had become a separate authority in 1996, and was now marking its boundaries accordingly. 'But all the traffic on that road will know it is going to York anyway,' said Colin.

'And these signs are as big as those on the motorways. They make no distinction between motorways and village lanes. There are 30 villages on the York authority boundary, and all those I have driven through are affected in the same way.'

Appleton Roebuck parishioners decided to negotiate with the City Council, and as a result a new sign has been designed for rural roads. It is a quarter of the original, and is a darker blue, with the reverse painted grey. 'We couldn't ask them to change the colour because they said blue was their corporate colour.' The new signs have not yet been erected but villagers hope they will arrive soon.

In Kent, too, some villages have awoken to find large bright yellow gateway signs, designed to tell drivers they are entering a village and should drive more slowly. Sandhurst, Linton and Sissinghurst were among the first to be installed and first to be disputed.

'Street furniture should be different in rural areas,' said Dan Clay, a CPRE supporter. 'Everything is standardised, from the kerbstones to the houses and the traffic signs. It makes everywhere look the same.'

No one disputes that traffic-calming measures are needed if the increase in traffic is to continue, but the fact that villages risk losing their good looks in the process has been given scant consideration. For example, sleeping policemen and other forms of traffic restraint are often accompanied by compulsory street lighting. Soon, thanks to the artificial 'skyglow', it will be impossible to see the stars except in very remote areas.

The small conservation village of Newnham in Kent now faces the twin problems of speed and lighting. Residents are desperate to stop cars roaring through their narrow main street on their way from Faversham to Sittingbourne.

'Drivers don't take account of the fact that it is a small village. Sometimes I find it difficult to hear my neighbour when we speak in our front gardens.' Said Dr Peter Gray, who lives in a small cottage on a road just wide enough for two cars.

'Kent County Council has been to see us and talked about chicanes and speed bumps but said we couldn't have anything unless we had street lighting first,' he said. 'But that would deny the whole character of the village.'

The sheer number of signs is increasing. This year the Government deregulated brown-and-white tourist signs, with the result that they have sprouted like weed-growth along the roadside. Few areas have been worse affected than the Lake District. 'They have just burgeoned,' said Dr Jan Darrall, a member of Friends of the Lake District.

'They pop up in places where it is already obvious exactly where the tourist attraction is, with advance warning signs two or three times along the way.' In consequence, if you wander lonely through Grasmere, where William Wordsworth lived and wrote his poetry, you come upon a host of . . . signs. Nowhere, it seems, is safe from the relentless advance of clutter in the countryside.

• *Cluttered Countryside*, by Caroline McGhie and Richard Girling, is published by the CPRE. Copies are available from CPRE, Warwick House, 25 Buckingham Palace Road, London. SW1W 0PP. Price £4.99 inc p&p.

Beating a rural retreat in the age of the City Kitty

By Steve Doughty, Social Affairs Correspondent

Tens of thousands are following the 'Laura Ashley' trail – seeking a clean, healthy life in the countryside.

They are the lucky ones wealthy and mobile enough to get away from polluted cities, according to a survey.

But behind them, they are leaving an ageing population where the family is breaking down and in future millions will live alone in ever-spreading suburbs.

The fragmented social strata are already highlighted in the fact that the number of pet cats has overtaken the dog population, because so many working couples and singles have nobody to look after a dog left at home all day.

The move from the cities, especially London, has become notable, according to *Social Trends*, the Government's annual look at national statistics. It shows the rural population has grown by 17 per cent since 1971, a change dubbed the 'Laura Ashley factor' by statisticians.

For years, the retired have headed for the countryside and for once-remote districts where numbers have been declining since Victorian times.

But now the successful middle classes are finding it possible to live away from the cities during their working lives, partly due to the advent of new technology.

Social Trends editor Jenny Church said: 'There is evidence that people will move out of the cities as soon as they can. Certainly they are leaving London.'

Plan for doubling size of English woodlands

Plans to transform the look of the English countryside by planting billions of trees and doubling the woodland cover of the land surface to 15 per cent are being launched by the Countryside and Forestry Commissions.

Large areas of unproductive farmland and derelict sites abandoned by mining and other industry are ear-marked for planting and Midland counties and Cornwall could become heavily wooded.

Plantings by the Forestry Commission, mostly of conifers, increased cover to 7.5 per cent but the Government is determined to double this to 15 per cent and has charged two Government quangos to get the scheme off the ground.

In a paper published today, the two organisations say determined action will be needed over many years to plant enough trees to cover 2.5 million acres of England which are currently bare of trees. This is in addition to the 12 community forests and the National Forest being planned close to towns and cities in England.

They say farmers are unschooled in growing trees and heavily dependent on short-term gains from crops paid for by the common agricultural policy. Reforms are needed and financial incentives to plant trees are necessary to get the scheme going.

They say the new landfill tax and lottery money may be tapped to get tree planting going.

Benefits would include new habitats, new opportunities for recreation, a boost to timber production, and an opportunity to revitalise degraded landscapes. More trees will help to reduce pollution and prevent global warming.

By Paul Brown, Environment Correspondent

Timber production is an important British industry worth about £12 billion in 1994 and employing around 34,000 people.

More trees will help to reduce pollution and prevent global warming

However, Britain imports 85 per cent of its timber. The idea is that most of the new timber planting will eventually produce a commercial return.

The two quangos' proposals are in a paper which asks for ideas and schemes to begin on the giant tree-planting scheme.

• *Woodland Creation* is available from the Countryside Commission, PO Box 124, Walgrave, Northampton, NN6 9TL. The publication is free of charge.

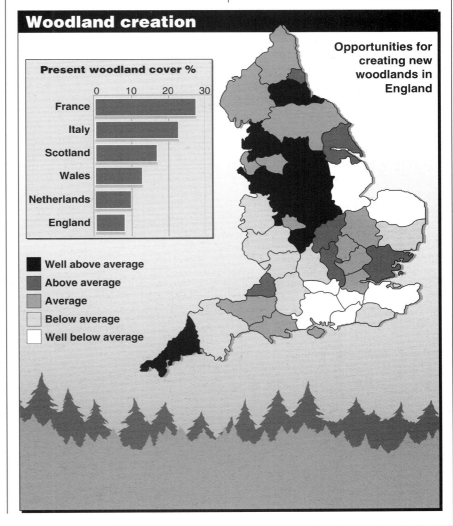

Woodland creation

Present woodland cover %

France
Italy
Scotland
Wales
Netherlands
England

0 10 20 30

Opportunities for creating new woodlands in England

■ Well above average
■ Above average
■ Average
□ Below average
□ Well below average

Tranquillity

A vanishing commodity

By Simon Rendel

You may yearn to get away from the rat-race and savour the peace and serenity of remote places, but in this crowded island is this a fanciful notion?

Since the earliest civilisations, people have been at odds in their outlook on life. On the one hand there are those fond of company, who need to communicate with others and relish the life of the city. On the other hand are the 'loners' whose individualism is played out on the remote frontier by the pioneer.

Between these two extremes, the great mass of people regard the prospect of being removed from other human beings with a variety of subtly different emotions – fear, longing, exhilaration, to name but a few. In this kaleidoscope one thing is certain – that, over time, any measure of the actual amount of remote landscape to be found on the planet will show an inexorable decline.

Until a century ago, only a few writers were sufficiently aware of the decline in frontier lands to express a romantic human need to seek out the remote. Explorers satisfied their personal needs by 'disappearing' into the bush in Africa, North and South America, Siberia and the Australian outback. They were the few because, concurrently, the great march to the cities and the suburbs was beginning.

As cities have grown and leisure time has expanded, a wider need to break away and find a pristine landscape untouched by urbanisation has begun to make itself felt. Yet, at the same time, that very landscape seems to have melted away, especially in western Europe, where the expansion of communications and energy has invaded an already densely-populated countryside.

Now people who regularly walk the English countryside are conscious of how much more difficult it is to plan a route away from roads, major pylon lines and suburban development – to find tranquil areas that are detached from urbanisation and town-living.

A scissors-shaped graph could be drawn up of the exponential rate of loss of remote countryside against a corresponding increase in demand for such countryside, showing the process to be doubly unsustainable. Not only that, with demand and loss working against each other, people have to travel further to reach remote countryside, thus decreasing the value of the landscape they travel through.

There are several ways in which this self-feeding process can be dampened. One is to concentrate all change in the areas already disturbed and ration access to travel corridors.

Another is to look for a reduction in population in order to offset the demand for space that comes with increased affluence.

Most laudable would be to encourage people to regard the resource of remote countryside as so important in a highly-populated land that visits to it should become an occasional privilege rather than a right for anyone at any time. Most patronising would be to encourage the less discriminating to appreciate pseudo-countryside, that is, countryside where recreation, as opposed to agriculture or wilderness, is dominant.

In theory it is possible to choose between inaction, action and muddling along; realistically, only the last will happen in the foreseeable future. This being the case, it is important to make sure that there exists a measure of the change that is taking place, and an awareness that this is only the beginning. Billions of

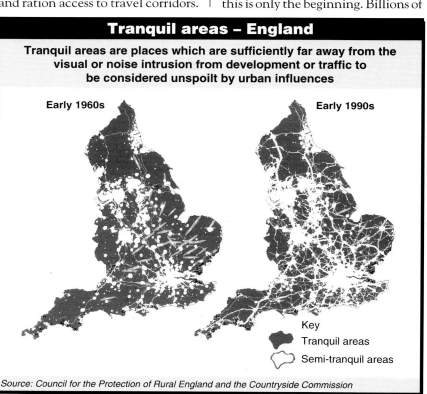

Tranquil areas – England

Tranquil areas are places which are sufficiently far away from the visual or noise intrusion from development or traffic to be considered unspoilt by urban influences

Early 1960s

Early 1990s

Key

Tranquil areas

Semi-tranquil areas

Source: Council for the Protection of Rural England and the Countryside Commission

people are still at the stage where the need to retreat to remoter landscapes is still dormant.

It is perhaps fortunate that we are only saddled with the memories of a few decades. Each generation will adjust to a degraded perception of what is remote, and Sir Ranulph Fiennes must settle for something different from Sir Richard Burton.

For myself and many others, the recollection of the countryside of southern England in the 50s is uppermost; I live with poignant memories of long walks unbroken by traffic intrusion and I must come to terms with both what has occurred and what is probably to come.

Unfortunately, such personal experience is still likely to be dismissed by a vocal – but, I hope, diminishing – minority, which sees any identification of the value of unspoilt countryside as stemming from, and reinforcing, privilege.

The extent and integrity of unspoilt countryside 30 years ago are evident for all to see on the Tranquil Area maps. The maps were created to provide the public, rather than academics, with an appreciation of change. In return, appreciation of them leaves me with some hope that the planning of 'ordinary' unspoilt countryside will be improved as public pressure comes to bear through a clearer understanding of the issues.

© Countryside
January/February, 1996

Living spaces

The common . . . priceless asset under threat

From vast sweeps of moorland to tiny green corners, there are no less than 8,675 areas defined as commons in England and Wales.

But they are poorly protected in law . . . at constant risk of enclosure or development. And, incredibly, we have no right to wander on 80 per cent of them.

The Open Spaces Society presses Parliament to recognise our right to walk freely over all commons . . . and wants to see caring management in place of neglect.

The green . . . vulnerable heart of the village

Village greens are the traditional hub of village life. But with uncertain legal protection, both village and town greens can all too easily succumb to roads, car parks and other encroachments.

The Open Spaces Society is the only body campaigning specifically to save the 3,000 greens of England and Wales . . . taking up cases and encouraging local action to protect them.

The urban space . . . so vital, we need more

As town dwellers, we desperately need our open spaces. Formal parks and recreation grounds, or the odd green patch which we enjoy . . . all make urban life more worth living.

But these spaces are vulnerable. Many are snapped up as development land. Others suffer from neglect and poor management.

The Open Spaces Society encourages local action to protect threatened spaces, and to turn derelict land into new recreation areas. And it campaigns for improved laws and policies to safeguard these spaces.

The footpath . . . a simple right worth saving

It may be a potentially valuable rural stroll, or just a handy short-cut. Either can get into trouble . . . blocked illegally, overgrown and neglected, or selfishly diverted.

When it happens, would-be rescuers turn to the Open Spaces Society for expert guidance on rights-of-way law, and experienced leads on the action to take.

Help us save them

Individuals, councils and local societies come to us whenever a common or other valued open space is in trouble. In a typically busy year we tackle more than 300 such cases, helping with experienced legal advice, authoritative literature and field officer backing for community action. A heavy commitment, and to keep offering help in all these cases, we need your help.

By joining, you strengthen our ability to save those areas you hold dear. As a member, you too can benefit from free advice whenever you need it. You get a lively, free magazine, *Open Space*, three times a year and member discounts on several valuable publications. Together, we can save those areas you hold dear.

A greater need than ever . . .

The Commons, Open Spaces and Footpaths Preservation Society, founded in 1865, was Britain's first national conservation body. In those early years we rescued such significant areas as Hampstead Heath, Epping Forest, Wimbledon and Berkhamsted Commons, from enclosure and development.

We won vital laws to protect metropolitan commons, to control fencing, to gain a public right to walk on urban commons, and to list commons on registers.

Our founders went on to create the National Trust. More recently we have pressed successfully for the recording of rights of way, and the designation of National Parks.

But the story continues. Far from resting on past successes, the Open Spaces Society, as we are known today, is campaigning to see thousands of rural commons and urban green spaces better managed, better protected and open for simple public enjoyment. It's a bigger-than-ever challenge for a small society, and to succeed we need your help.

• The above information is produced by the Open Spaces Society. See page 39 for address details.
© *The Open Spaces Society*

People abandon cities for the country life

Study shows that Government attempts to revitalise urban areas have failed to stem the tide of migration to rural towns and villages

It was billed as an illustration of academic vitality and the relevance of the social sciences. Yesterday, the Economic and Social Research Council, the country's largest independent funder of research in the field, released a series of studies to coincide with the publication of its annual report.

Attempts to revitalise urban Britain have failed as large numbers of residents continue to abandon cities for rural areas, according to research published yesterday.

More than 1.25 million people left Britain's six largest metropolitan areas between 1991 and 1994, equivalent to a net loss of 90,000 a year.

The research, based on data generated by the 1991 census and the NHS central register, will come as worrying news for the Government which last week announced that 60 per cent of new homes should be built in cities in an attempt to stem the flow of people moving to the countryside.

Tony Champion, a geographer at Newcastle University who conducted the study, said it confirmed fears that Britain's cities were shrinking. Despite decades of initiatives designed to make urban life more attractive, he found people were moving down the 'urban hierarchy' from large cities to towns down to villages.

> ### *More than 1.25 million people left Britain's six largest metropolitan areas between 1991 and 1994, equivalent to a net loss of 90,000 a year*

'There is a clear cascade effect with each tier of the hierarchy receiving inflows from the tier above.'

While all cities experienced net losses, London suffered most, with a net loss of more than 628,000 – equivalent to double the size of Coventry's population. It was the most rural areas which showed the highest net increases.

Prof Champion said the effect of this exodus on London's population may have been masked by a higher-than-average birth-rate as well as absorbing most immigration into Britain. 'But it was certainly not masked from the point of view of the countryside where the pressure of increased numbers is very evident.'

Elsewhere, where there was less immigration, cities were forced to rely solely on births to shore up their populations as older residents left.

The West Midlands conurbation, which covers Birmingham, lost more than 220,000 residents over the 14-year period, while Greater Manchester lost more than 123,000.

The only group moving into urban areas in greater numbers than they had been leaving were 16 to 29-year-olds. But there was evidence that even they would choose more rural locations once they were older. The 30 to 44-year-olds showed a particularly strong desire to leave the big cities.

© *The Guardian*
December, 1996

Household growth

Where shall we live?

In launching his White Paper, the Environment Secretary has grasped a very emotional issue. However, some of the difficulties associated with it have been grossly exaggerated.

Far from being such a big problem, the scale of need is not particularly dramatic and should be relatively easy to deal with. We will need to build up to 200,000 houses per year in England. That compares with 3.5 million houses that were built in the 1960s, three million in the 1970s and only two million in the 1980s. So this is actually part of a dramatic slowing down in rates of housebuilding over 30 years.

Relatively harmless numbers have taken on a demonic quality while much more important issues that we should be debating have been overlooked.

Families matter

Despite the concentration on single people in the projections, families will remain very important. It is illogical for politicians to express concern about families, while ignoring the provision of proper housing for them. Equally, it is wrong to treat single-person households as an homogeneous group and to assume they want small houses or flats. They are clearly very diverse and are geographically wide-spread. Single first-time buyers are leap-frogging the market, wherever they can, to buy larger houses. They want more space, wherever they can get it. No 'neat-fit', pushing them all into high density urban areas, is remotely realistic.

Improve urban life

Householders have been the largest agents of urban regeneration for over 40 years. But setting them unrealistic targets for levels of urban development is short-term political expediency of the worst kind.

We cannot turn our urban areas into dustbins for the shire county NIMBYs (Not In My Back Yard). We cannot destroy the quality of life in our towns and cities by cramming these people into the urban areas so that more people will try to leave, putting more pressure on the edges of the towns and suburbs.

You cannot improve the quality of life in our urban areas overnight. You need better medium-term plans for education, employment, and dealing with crime. You certainly do not achieve it by cramming high-density housing into every available space.

Furthermore, not only will household growth be greatest in counties that are not adjacent to brownfield sites, but such sites will become more difficult to find. As the economy improves, they may not be developed for housing at all, because other uses will give better values to their owners. And how can using every site for housing be reconciled with greening the cities?

Where to build?

We must search for suitable new land on the edge of towns. There should be a fine sift of all the rough and damaged fields, surrounded on three sides by development, bounded by main roads etc. Then we should look at the business and retail parks, for example, that have been developed in recent years. Land there is already developed, whether it should have been or not, and it has roads and sewers, often with spare capacity. Many of these would make ideal cores for sustainable development.

People want to be close to shops, schools, jobs, and entertainment. But many people think housebuilders want to build on the 24 million acres of agricultural land in the UK. The vast majority of people do not want to live in the 'countryside'. It is miles from anywhere: it is too expensive to build infrastructure and no one would buy the houses. So no housebuilder in his right mind wants to build there.

Put people first

We must put the people – not statistics, acres of land – at the centre of this debate. They are people, not households. They want enough space in the right location. We must be concerned about their quality of life and what we leave behind for the future. We need innovative ways of linking transport, housing, schools, retailing and jobs to produce more long-term sustainable patterns of development. The minister has to start the debate because local decision-makers have capitulated to NIMBYism. Whoever wins the General Election will have to start acting strategically to improve the living environment of our people, and not simply to prevent change.

© House Builders' Federation
January, 1997

Towns to grow in green fields

Countryside at risk: millions of homes needed

ields will disappear under bricks and concrete if land is to be found for the millions of homes needed for a growing number of households, a major study revealed yesterday.

The Government estimates that almost 4.5 million new homes are needed over the next 20 years. But an investigation into where they may be built reveals a mismatch between demand and supply of land – and this could have a dramatic effect on the landscape of southern England.

As people continue to leave the cities, planners say that 'large-scale use' of undeveloped land is 'inevitable'.

Their study, produced by the Town and Country Planning Association and the Joseph Rowntree Trust, warns that while the Government policy of using former industrial sites for development means that half of all housing is now built on recycled or 'brownfield' land, this will decline in the years ahead.

Professor Peter Hall, of University College, London, who co-edited the report, said that the pressure to move out of cities 'threatens current policies which encourage sustainable, environmentally sensitive development'.

By Charlie Bain

Demand for land in the south-east is strongest west of London, but most former industrial land lies to the east. In the north-west, land is available in Manchester and Liverpool but most new housing is needed in Cheshire, Cumbria and rural Lancashire. In Yorkshire and Humberside demand is in the north – but most brownfield sites are in South Yorkshire.

> **As people continue to leave the cities, planners say that 'large-scale use' of undeveloped land is 'inevitable'**

Solutions to finding enough land, says the report, include spreading into protected green-belt countryside, building along rail corridors, filling vacant sites within urban areas and creating new villages and towns.

Tony Burton, a senior planner with the Council for the Protection of Rural England (CPRE), said: 'Commitment to urban renewal should be the starting-point in the debate.'

It is significant that the idea of new towns has returned, after nearly a decade of intense opposition exemplified by anger over plans to build over Foxley Wood in Berkshire.

Now new towns are on the drawing-board for Hampshire, Kent, Berkshire, Essex, Hertfordshire, East Sussex, Cambridgeshire, Cheshire, Gloucestershire and Devon, plus 'bolt-on' settlements next to Bristol, Swindon, Peterborough, Dorchester, Dartford and Glasgow.

In January a £500m 'bolt-on' new town complete with 5,500 homes, to be built next to Peterborough, was announced by the Hanson Trust. In Hampshire, Eagle Star have drawn up plans to build an 8,000-home new town at Micheldever, on 1,000 acres of arable land beside the main railway line from Southampton to Waterloo.

© *The Independent*
August, 1996

Why village England wants to be kept in dark

Campaigners call for action over growing light pollution. By Barbie Dutter

At 2 am in north-west London, a confused songbird perches on a streetlamp, trilling and twittering as if it were dawn. It is night, yet it is light. Few stars punctuate the amber glow that suffuses the sky.

In vast tracts of urban and suburban England, nightfall is no longer synonymous with darkness. And, increasingly, the problem of intrusive artificial light is spilling into rural areas.

Snaking orange ribbons, created by the light from six million road-lamps, carve through the countryside. Floodlit sports grounds, trigger-happy security systems and cathedrals and monuments bathed in night-time brightness have all contributed to the growing clamour over light pollution.

Yesterday, at the first conference of its kind, campaigners outlined their case for less light at night and called for government action to curb the problem.

They were encouraged by the keynote address of the Environment Secretary, John Gummer, who pledged to explore 'any workable measures' to tackle their concerns.

'In this country we value the safety and security lighting brings, and the contribution it makes to the quality of life,' he said. 'However, problems of bad lighting are getting through. We need to look at the current framework of legislation and guidance to see if we can deal with these problems more effectively.'

The British Astronomical Association launched its Dark Skies Campaign six years ago, but the problem of 'sky glow' was first pinpointed by astronomers in the mid-seventies, when a surge in outdoor lighting followed the end of the 1974 energy crisis.

The nineties have seen an even greater proliferation. The Millennium Commission has been inundated with bids for grandiose floodlighting schemes for bridges, docks, historic buildings, parks and even office blocks.

> ### In vast tracts of urban and suburban England, nightfall is no longer synonymous with darkness

Astronomers, environmental groups and romantics alike are alarmed by the number and scale of such projects, pointing out that the light from cities already brightens night skies up to 50 miles away.

Britain is one of the most brightly lit countries in Europe, according to a satellite map of Europe produced by the BAA. Only Belgium and the Netherlands are more illuminated.

John Mason, the association's vice president, said: 'The issue is not any longer just the province of astronomers. The orange glow that hides the view of the stars is only one aspect of lighting pollution.'

A recent survey showed that most local authorities had received complaints about intrusive or excessive lighting, particularly relating to security systems, sports facilities and decorative flood-lighting.

The Council for the Protection of Rural England has, for the last two years, been vociferous on the subject. Sian Phipps, the CPRE's land use campaigner, said: 'Darkness at night is one of the most precious resources that the countryside has left.

'Dark nights, star-studded skies, moonlight shadows and the shades of dusk and dawn are as much a part of the character and quality of the countryside as its mosaic of trees and hedgerows, mountains and moorlands.

'Some areas of the South-East are completely obliterated. There are parts which are lit up 24 hours a day, where people don't know what it's like to look up and see the stars.

'We mustn't allow intrusive light to erode our reservoirs of darkness. It is disruptive to wildlife and a great disturbance to the human soul. The distinction between daylight and darkness gives us a very measured balance to our days, months and even our yearly cycle.'

Light is not officially recognised as a pollutant and there is no proper regulatory framework for it in Britain, nor any recourse for those suffering from it. Often, no planning permission is required for lighting sports facilities and amenities.

© Telegraph Group Limited, London 1996

Urban footprints

The future of our countryside depends on our towns and cities treading more lightly on the environment

Benefits of city development

High-quality urban development makes the best use of scarce land resources – increases the cost effectiveness of public transport – reduces the loss of countryside – provides a positive alternative to building which damages landscapes and habits – maintains urban populations – supports urban facilities and services – reduces the need for car travel – is more energy efficient – provides opportunities to live without a car or be less dependent on it – reduces length of journeys – improves the local environment of the vast majority of the population – tackles the problem of urban dereliction – provides homes where people live – revitalises vacant buildings – returns unfit homes to active use – supports existing business investments – makes positive use of empty offices and vacant industrial land – improves town centres – supports existing infrastructure.

The choice before us

Every day hundreds of people move out of our cities to live in rural towns and villages. Rural land is consumed by new housing, roads, shopping centres and commercial development. Car use is spiralling upwards and journeys are getting longer. Meanwhile we are failing to get the best out of our cities. Thousands of acres of urban land lie derelict and tens of thousands of buildings remain vacant.

This is a picture of how we are exploiting our land – the most valuable resource in this small and overcrowded country. The distinction between town and country is becoming blurred and we are wasting scarce resources.

COUNCIL FOR THE
PROTECTION OF
RURAL ENGLAND

CPRE believes these trends cannot continue. The vital resource which our countryside represents for us all risks being lost forever while our cities increasingly stand as monuments to neglect.

People's desire to live and work in the countryside is not surprising. People are more mobile than they have ever been and the attractions of rural life are obvious. But we cannot all move out to the country any more than we can give up on the generations of human investment in the fabric of our cities. To accept these trends as inevitable would be to condemn both urban and rural England to a poorer environment.

Development and change are of course necessary in rural areas but the scale of current building pressures is much too high. For example, we need to provide hundreds of thousands of new homes in England just to meet the requirements of the current population; but since nearly 80% of the population live in towns and cities this is where we should focus most of our efforts. The countryside cannot and need not carry the weight of continuing dispersal.

The challenge is to find ways of meeting society's needs and aspirations without continually building over our countryside. We should make better use of the infrastructure we already have. Land use and planning policies for town and country should be considered together and patterns of new development encouraged which make best use of the land and other resources in both. We should celebrate and enhance all that makes cities attractive and provide people with a positive alternative to leaving town – a high-quality urban environment in which to live.

Urban footprints

All new development – urban or rural – has an impact on land and resources. The impact of a new housing estate extends far beyond the site where it is built. It can be traced to the quarries supplying the building bricks, the reservoirs providing the water for people's taps and the landfill sites absorbing the rubbish. Its new residents will make different types of journeys to work or to the shops. This may put more cars on the roads or add to the pressure to widen them.

The nature and size of the 'footprint' generated by these and other impacts depend crucially on where and how the development takes place. We need to find policies and incentives to ensure new building takes place where its 'footprint' treads most lightly on the environment. In many places this can bring environmental improvements.

Focusing on the way we use and develop our cities is a crucial part of the answer. They are the source of most of the pressure for new development. But encouraging more and better-quality development to locate in urban areas will require a renewed commitment by all those involved – central and local government, developers, pension funds and other investors – as well as the support of an active public.

Town cramming and tower blocks?

The environmental 'footprint' of our cities can be reduced without a return to 1960s' tower blocks or the loss of important open space.

Tower blocks offer few environmental advantages and can have a damaging effect on urban communities. Despite appearances, high-rise blocks frequently house people at a lower density than the housing they replaced. Higher density development can be provided by converting existing houses or building new homes in low-rise mixed-facility developments. Family homes can still have gardens and the street environment can be improved.

Open spaces are vital to the urban environment. Parks, playing fields and fragments of woodland in our cities need not be sacrificed for

The impact of a new housing estate extends far beyond the site where it is built

new building. Even if they were all developed they could only provide a fraction of our building needs but at a huge environmental and social cost. The bulk of new development should come from making better use of existing built-up areas and run-down land. Open land and urban wildspace make urban living more attractive and provide an alternative to the long trek to the countryside.

Vibrant cities

Our cities present a planning conundrum. On the one hand they have the potential to house, employ, transport and support large numbers of people efficiently. On the other they contain large areas of wasted land and empty buildings and unnecessarily consumed natural resources.

The bulk of the houses, factories, offices, shopping centres and other developments needed by England's 46 million people needs to be provided in towns and cities. However desirable the countryside is as a place to live it could never accommodate all the needs of modern society without losing its own value to society – its identity, its value for recreation and relaxation, and its ability to produce agricultural products in an environ-mentally responsible way. This has already been recognised in strong Green Belt and other planning policies which have helped keep England's urban areas relatively compact and protected much agri-cultural land

from development. So although we have problems, we also have a foundation on which to build a fresh approach for the twenty-first century.

But despite their advantages we are not making good use of our cities. The urban environment is too often blighted by empty homes, vacant buildings and derelict land. There is not enough investment in reclamation and reuse of land or buildings and cities lack the transport facilities they deserve. And planning and other land-use policies for urban areas are too often geared to outdated thinking about car parking standards and building density which obstruct regeneration efforts.

High-quality urban development can bring real advantages for our cities, the countryside, and the wider environment. Revitalising the city does not have to mean a return to tower blocks or the sacrifice of important open space. High density, low-rise development can provide a high-quality environment. Given the opportunity, our cities can constantly renew themselves and provide more capacity for new development than is often appreciated. Research for the Joseph Rowntree Foundation, for example, showed that even quite modest changes to current practice could double the capacity for housing development of the areas studied. Planners need to embrace the possibilities brought by higher density housing development and a reduced dependence on the car.

We should celebrate the positive things about urban life – the built environment and the social, economic and cultural opportunities it provides – and do more to protect what remains of the green space in our towns. We need a new approach: a new optimism about the value to society of our towns and cities and a new determination to invest in them for the benefit of us all – today and in the future.

What can be done?

There is a lot we can do for our cities. Here are a few suggestions, showing how everyone has a role to play in improving the quality of our urban areas and protecting the countryside:

The Government
- refine planning controls, policies and tax incentives so as to encourage builders and businesses to focus on urban areas
- allow local authorities to do more to tackle vacancy and dereliction
- provide more funds
- issue planning guidance on cities and sustainability
- set national and regional objectives for reducing the rate of loss of countryside to new building

- discourage those who hoard vacant land and buildings

Local councils
- plan positively for every part of urban England
- remove obstacles (e.g. restrictive parking standards, maximum density policies) to the better use of urban land
- support community-based solutions
- help bring development to where it is needed
- protect networks of open space
- improve local leisure provision
- safeguard town centres
- provide employment, shopping and other facilities in suburban areas which do not have them
- provide pedestrian priority and car-free areas

Developers, landowners and commerce
- underpin the benefits of past investment in town centres
- contribute to the management of urban spaces and provision of public facilities for both economic and environmental reasons
- respond to the opportunities provided by Government regeneration initiatives

- refurbish and convert as alternatives to new-build
- release vacant land
- avoid car-based development

Public services
- improve urban public transport
- provide high-quality local health care and education
- tie future strategies more closely to land-use plans

People
- press local councils and your MP for new policies and funds to improve the urban environment
- prepare community strategies for your neighbourhood
- highlight areas of dereliction and decay and opportunities for enhancement and development
- demand a positive response
- celebrate the positive aspects of city life

• The above is an extract from *Urban Footprints*, produced by the Council for the Protection of Rural England (CPRE). See page 39 for address details.

© CPRE
November, 1994

Why I should be stopped from fleeing to suburbia

Nicholas Schoon on a pernicious middle-class exodus

I want to live in the countryside one day. But now I live in the suburbs, with my wife and three children who will probably leave home within the next 15 years and set up households of their own. I imagine that they, like their parents, won't marry and have children until their late twenties or early thirties (if at all). And I want to live to a ripe old age.

I and my family are squarely part of a huge environmental problem: the disappearance of an area

of English countryside the size of Greater London, buried under new housing within the next 20 years. That is what is implied by the

The population is growing slowly, but the number of households is expected to shoot up by nearly a quarter by 2016

Government's forecast for an extra 4.4 million households to be formed between 1991 and 2016, even if half of the new homes required are built within existing towns, cities and villages.

The population is growing slowly, but the number of households is expected to shoot up by nearly a quarter by 2016. This is because we are living longer, marrying later, splitting up more frequently and much more likely to live alone. Yesterday the Department of the

Environment published a consultation paper about where, in this crowded country, all those homes should go. It agonised over these issues, asked lots of pertinent questions, and in the end committed itself to discussing targets, but not to policies to achieve them.

At the moment, I can't afford my dream country home anywhere near my work in London, nor face the prospect of the extra commuting. So I live in the most suburban of outer London suburbs, a few hundred yards from where the ranks of inter-war semis (just like mine) abruptly give way to Green Belt.

I'd like to live nearer the heart of the capital. We did, for seven years, and we enjoyed it – a small Edwardian terrace, the big and little parks nearby, the bustle and variety and the short journey to work. But when the time came for our eldest child to go to secondary school, we checked the Government's league tables and moved from Greenwich to Bromley, where children get a lot more qualifications. We had no confidence in our nearest inner-city comprehensive and no chance of getting him in the better one a little further away. So like millions of middle-class parents who can't afford or don't want their children to go to private schools, we fled to the anodyne suburbs.

We felt bad, knowing this kind of behaviour makes for inner-city decline. But, as Tony Blair and Harriet Harman tell us, your children come first, and unlike those MPs we could find no way of getting our son

---

Both central and local government seem resigned to the fact that few people with money, jobs and children will want to live in inner cities

---

into a good inner-city school.

If the Government is serious about stopping both urban decline and ever-growing suburban sprawl across the diminishing countryside, it should have no higher priority than improving schools near the centres of big towns and cities. But this gets only the briefest mention in the housing paper from the Environment Secretary.

Raising inner-city school standards is difficult and expensive. Both central and local government seem resigned to the fact that few people with money, jobs and children will want to live in inner cities. Yet politicians of all parties wish for the centres to be inhabited by people other than the left-behind poor, in order to keep the urban heart beating.

So they warm to the idea of students, young singles, childless marrieds and old people living in smaller homes in the core of cities. The children of the self-sufficient are to be raised in John Major's 'invincible green suburbs'. Once they grow up, they will move into the city centres to work and study, and it is

being suggested that it would be a good idea if their newly alone parents did so, too.

But the parents will probably still want to retire to a cottage in the countryside. And their children, too, will wish to move out of the centre when they have children, unless the schools do get better – and the city streets safer. By the time they do move, there will be numerous big new suburbs for them to live in, in places that are now fields and woods.

This unceasing sprawl does not only erase the countryside, a national asset which most people treasure. Dispersed, low-density 'burbs' are hard to service by public transport and they encourage the car culture, with its attendant pollution and congestion.

If we are to slow the outward march of suburbia, people such as myself must be stopped from achieving our dream of country living. The supply of new housing in greenfield sites must be so limited that out-of-town house prices become prohibitive. Meanwhile, homes should be built on derelict and vacant land in the cities, created in the empty space above shops and in out-of-date offices. For once we – the comfortable, middle-class English – know we are fated to raise our families and end our days in town, we will make it a fit place to live in. The politicians have to summon the courage to make us give up our dreams and start us planning our un-English urban future.

© *The Independent*
November, 1996

Urban development

Trends of modern society

The conference explored many of the trends of modern society which are fundamental to the work of planners, architects and all those involved in urban development today. What emerged strongly was that in a new world of globalisation, local communities are more important than ever and under greater threat. Urban development must respond to these changes.

The trends

- Despite population stability or even decline in the UK over the next 20 years, the number of households is predicted to rise by 4.4 million, an increase of 23%.
- This is primarily due to a massive rise in the number of single-person households, accounting for 80% of the growth.
- This increase is due to a number of factors: the rising divorce rate, young people leaving home earlier, women increasingly economically able to live alone.

The world of work

- The Western world is experiencing a shift to a post-industrial, information-age society. The growth sectors are concentrated in the service sector, notably financial services and the caring professions.
- The nature of work is changing with greater flexibility of employment, rising part-time and temporary work and self-employment. The job for life is replaced by the likelihood that most people will experience a period of unemployment.
- Young people today are likely to need to reskill completely during their working life. Trainability and employability become far more important with the death of a career for life.
- There will be a polarisation between the information-rich

> *Despite population stability or even decline in the UK over the next 20 years, the number of households is predicted to rise by 4.4 million*

and the information-poor, both in terms of people and in terms of regions and countries.

Technological change

- Technological change will impact on urban life through a series of competing factors. These include: telecommunications versus transportation; electronic services versus material goods; virtual venues versus physical places.
- These factors will have a decentralising effect, as has been experienced to a lesser extent with the car and the telephone.
- People and companies will be more mobile and planners need to work harder to attract a retain human capital through creating pleasant living places.

The changes taking place need to be considered in the context of their impact on the urban fabric. It is only through understanding those impacts that our own towns and cities can effectively respond to them.

Impact on the urban fabric

Leisure

- Workers can increasingly expect to experience periods of unemployment during their working life.
- Lower retirement ages and longer life expectancy mean that people are retiring and still enjoying several years of active life.
- People need identities, and if they cannot have identity through employment, new creative roles must be found.

Creating communities

- At a time when work was dirty and dangerous, the early New Towns recognised the need to separate work and living space to improve the quality of life.
- More recently the changing nature of work has made that separation unnecessary. The evolution of the New Towns saw the convergence of work and residence.
- Today the value of mixed-use development is widely recognised.
- There is evidence that within a city the higher the volume of traffic, the greater the separation between individuals and households; people need real civic space.

Technological change

- Functions that were previously carried out in a town centre will increasingly be done in the home, such as Internet banking and shopping.
- Buildings such as high-street banks are now redundant and alternative uses must be found. Notably, banks have been converted into restaurants, pubs and wine bars, having a positive impact on the night-time economy.
- Predicted increases in self-employment and home working require housing which incorporates these roles and communities that respond to the blurring of home and work space.
- In order to take advantage of the opportunities of technological change, local communities need to be enabled to access these opportunities.

There has been much recent discussion about the predicted demand for 4.4 million dwellings over the next 20 years. This conference was particularly concerned to look at this issue. The Secretary of State for the Environment launched his 'Great Debate' at the conference, calling for real public discussion on where these new homes should go.

The future

Future housing demand

- Housing design needs to take into account a range of factors in order to respond to changes taking place.
- Housing needs to reflect the increase in flexible and home working and rising self-employment.
- Although the increased demand for accommodation is mainly by single people, many have relationships which divide their time between their separated parents.
- Spacious housing is the key to these things and others, such as caring for elderly relatives.

Sustainable development

- The environmental impact of traffic, particularly private cars, means that sustainable development should be developed with lower reliance on cars.
- Sustainable development also requires that future development should take place on brown field sites where possible and green field sites should be conserved.
- Sustainability requires investment in efficient public transport systems and environmentally friendly buildings.
- Technological change will have positive environmental effects: information services can replace scarce material resources, such as paper; electronic access to work cuts travel requirements.

Within the global economy, dangers of polarisation and social exclusion have been much discussed. Planners of the New Towns such as Ebenezer Howard understood the fundamental role played by planning and breaking and urban design in making communities. The thinkings behind the New Towns has much to inform us in meeting the housing demands today.

- The above is an extract from a conference paper *Today's Opportunities, Tomorrow's Visions*, published by the Commission for the New Towns. See page 39 for address details.

© *Commission for the New Towns*

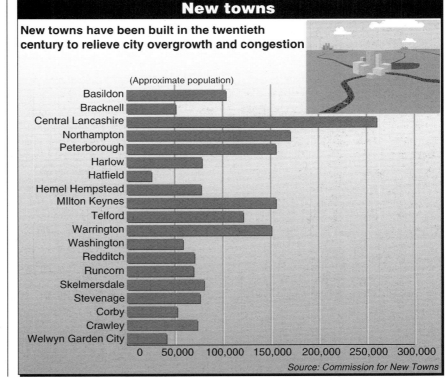

New towns

New towns have been built in the twentieth century to relieve city overgrowth and congestion

(Approximate population)

Source: Commission for New Towns

London's calling

What would it take to make a city sustainable? An integrated and far-sighted approach to planning, at the very least. Martin Wright looks at a future ripe with possibilities, aimed at shifting London in the right direction

London is calling, and it sounds like a Mayday – a distress signal from a city which is almost an object lesson in unsustainability. London has some of the worst air quality in Western Europe, the heftiest traffic jams, and none of the city-wide strategic planning essential for such a metropolis. A recent survey found that 81% of Londoners felt that 'urgent action' was needed to improve the city's environment. So what will it take to make London sustainable?

Street life

London's public transport network is one of the most expensive, and least efficient, of any metropolis. On the streets, central London traffic speeds average a paltry 8 mph – exactly the same as a century ago. And motor vehicles are the leading cause of pollution. This is set against excellent rail and air links to the outside world. London is easy to access, but tough to traverse.

As a first step, say campaigners, turn transport priorities on their head. Design streets to discourage car use, and favour pedestrians, cyclists, and public transport – in that order. Consider car bans on high streets. Cut speed limits to 20 mph – thereby, ironically, increasing average speeds across the capital. Cut car parking spaces on city streets; convert car parks to social housing. Reduce the capacity of the road network and green 'spare' highway space. Use tax incentives to encourage home delivery schemes and corner shops. Design new estates as car-free zones. Ensure secure cycle parks and workplace storage. Boost investment in the Tube.

'Business needs a decent transport infrastructure,' says Amy Kroviak, policy co-ordinator of the CBI's London region. 'We need to get people to work on time. And that means addressing the massive backlog in investment on the underground.' London First, of which the CBI is a member, is calling for £700 million over the next few years.

Integrated transport is the key. 'You have to make it easy for people to switch between cars, tubes and trains,' says Herbert Girardet, an environmentalist who specialises in the 'metabolism' of cities. Roads freed of traffic would be open to new types of 'taxi-bus' hybrid vehicles: light, fast minibuses to link residential areas with shopping and business centres.

Streets for humans

But improving transport alone is only part of the picture. Rehumanizing the street means planning for a different urban structure. Girardet suggests planning authorities should actively encourage 'urban village' developments, mixing residential with workshop and office space, allowing people to live and work in the same vicinity. Energy-efficient conversions of redundant office buildings, or redevelopments on the 5% of London's land which is effectively derelict, would be a plus.

In its manifesto, *Creating a Sustainable London*, the Sustainable London Trust calls for new 'low-impact' mini-neighbourhoods, with features such as co-operative self-build housing, passive solar design and photo-voltaic cladding for energy efficiency; an 'eco-floor' on the roof for greenhouse gardening; permaculture plots in place of car parks; and mini-workshops for residents. The trust also suggests 'right to repair' schemes, allowing council estate residents to carry out their own maintenance with appropriate training, while 'sensible squatter' schemes could allow semi-derelict or hard-to-rent housing to be occupied by enterprising young people.

A power in the city

London is a voracious consumer of energy. Per capita, its consumption is higher than almost all its European equivalents. Ageing office and residential buildings guzzle power, while even new developments often lack sophisticated energy-efficient design. Curious as to the proportion of energy wasted by its residents, the London Borough of Ealing carried out an infra-red survey of selected streets. The findings were chilling in more ways than one: over 60% of home heating was being lost through inadequately insulated windows, doors, walls and roofs. A sizeable proportion of householder expenditure was being used to heat the skies above Ealing's streets. Overall only one in 12 of the capital's houses meets the energy efficiency standards required for new buildings.

There are rewards to be reaped from improving this figure. Overall, Girardet says, London's consumption of 20 mtoe (million tonnes of oil equivalent) per annum could be cut by 50% by a combination of existing technology and demand-side management. In the immediate term, the construction of a series of CHP (combined heat-and-power) plants would result in significant savings. Such plants make use of the waste heat created in electricity generation, to warm local homes and offices. A newly opened CHP plant in Smithfield is providing heating and chilled water for air-conditioning to the Barbican and nearby city buildings. In Copenhagen, for example, over 90% of the city's energy is generated by CHPs.

The Sustainable London Trust favours specially designed micro-industrial developments based around CHP plants. Glasshouses growing vegetables for the capital could be heated by a nearby CHP station. The Lea Valley, whose greenhouses have lost out to cheap food flown in from abroad, could be revitalised by such a scheme, argues Girardet. 'Some of the highest unemployment rates in the country are in the Lea Valley,' he points out, 'and yet a new power station at Nazeing [10 miles north-east of London] has a cooling tower pumping heat into the air, surrounded by greenhouses whose owners are struggling to pay their heating bills. It's an opportunity squandered.'

In the longer term, photovoltaic (PV) cladding – which is gradually emerging as an economically viable technology – could make a major contribution. Studies suggests that about 10% of London's buildings could be self-sufficient in electricity during daylight hours. There are a variety of ways in which new buildings could be encouraged to adopt such important energy-saving techniques.

London's rubbish

London is literally a wasteful city. It recycles around 5% of its rubbish – one of the lowest rates in Europe. If current trends continue, it hasn't a hope of meeting the Government's 25% target by the turn of the century. But hope is at hand. London Pride, the alliance of business, local authorities and other London NGOs, has launched a Waste Action Programme designed to turn the city's rubbish into a resource. With the help of a £12 million Capital Challenge grant, the programme is working with London boroughs on a series of pilot schemes aimed at meeting the 25% target for household rubbish, and increasing it to 40% by 2005. Strategies vary, but in broad terms it means running a weekly collection for most recyclable wastes – glass, paper, steel, aluminium, textiles, and, eventually, plastics, organic waste for composting, and electronic components. Four boroughs – Hounslow, Hackney, Haringey and Enfield – are currently taking part in the pilots, while one scheme in Ealing is already

---

London is literally a wasteful city. It recycles around 5% of its rubbish – one of the lowest rates in Europe

---

succeeding in recycling 45% of household waste.

Long term, says the Programme Director, Robin Murray, recycling will help to regenerate London. 'At the moment, virtually every industry which uses recycled materials – whether paper, plastics or textiles – tells us it has a problem with supply. So the demand's there. This can be a demand-led exercise.' One possibility is for a series of small-scale paper mills, using the latest 'closed loop' clean production processes, powered by CHP, on the banks of rivers such as the Lea.

The key is to bring the industry close to the supply of raw materials. Murray envisages a series of small factories supplying London with everything from high-grade plastic products to art paper, using the city's own waste as their main feedstock. London's sewage, dumped at sea until the practice was banned by the EU, will now be incinerated: a gross waste of a valuable agricultural resource, says the Sustainable London Trust. It points to Bristol, whose sewage is transformed into granules of fertilizer and used to help reclaim the sterile slag heaps of South Wales.

Is anyone in charge?

London's lack of a central authority is widely identified as a major stumbling-block. There's a Minister for London (currently Environment Secretary John Gummer) chairing a Cabinet sub-committee. And there's the Government Office for London, which in theory co-ordinates relevant activities of various departments. But neither these, nor the Association of London Government, which groups the borough authorities, has the sort of overarching strategic planning powers seen as essential.

Many see the future in a London-wide strategic authority – indeed, the Labour Party is committed to reintroducing one. The Sustainable London Trust says such an authority should enshrine sustainability as an organising principle, and have the power to raise a rate via the boroughs. Local eco-taxes, on car parking spaces, for example, could be levied to fund specific initiatives, such as energy efficiency.

But the real trick is ensuring active participation by Londoners. The Trust advocates neighbourhood forums to encourage as wide as possible participation in local initiatives. This would feed into a 'London Citizen's Forum', which would both co-ordinate information about sustainability initiatives and act as a citizen's advocate to any London government.

'Citizen's groups have more imagination than local authorities,' says Herbert Girardet. 'We need an elected authority with an inbuilt commitment to sustainable development, but we also need to activate the creativity of Londoners.'

But can London really be turned around? Robin Clement, Deputy Chief Planner at LPAC, strikes a grimly realistic note. 'There's a long way to go before strategic planning policies can really deliver a more sustainable London,' he says. 'We all say we want a better environment, but in the end many of us continue to use our cars. We've not yet captured the hearts and minds of individual Londoners.'

London's woefully inefficient energy and transport infrastructure may consume vast quantities of natural resources, but in human terms it is an immensely resourceful city. 'There's a wealth of ingenuity available, from taxi drivers to financiers to admen,' says Girardet. 'And there are more environmental groups in London than any other city on earth. Together, they make a tremendous resource which could be harnessed to help their home city.'

• Martin Wright is Commissioning Editor of *Green Futures* and a regular contributor to *Tomorrow Magazine*.
© Green Futures Publications
April/May, 1997

Super-cities threaten to swallow humanity

Developing world hosts explosive urban growth. By John Lichfield

The entire globe is following the nineteenth-century European and American example and pouring into cities, with implications that could be either benign or calamitous.

Within 10 years the majority of the people of the world will be living in urban conglomerations, the United Nations reported yesterday. Almost all the urban growth will come in the developing world, which is spawning large cities at the rate of 10 a year.

In 1950 the world had 83 cities with populations of 1,000,000 or more (about the size of Birmingham or Glasgow). Today there are 280. By 2015 there will be more than 500.

By the year 2015, 12 of the world's 15 largest cities will be in Asia; only one – New York – will be in North America; none will be in Europe.

In 1950, only one city – New York – had a population of more than 10 million. Now there are 14, of which only four are in the developed world. Early in the next century, only one European city – greater Paris – will be in the world's top 30. Lagos will be the third largest city in the world.

From ancient Rome to nineteenth-century New York or Manchester, cities have always been ambiguous institutions. They have been sinks of crime, depravity, oppression, poverty and suffering. But they have also been crucibles of personal enrichment, civilisation, culture and political rights. The UN says the vast urbanisation in progress has, similarly, a potential for immense social progress and economic advance and a capacity for disaster and human degradation on an unimaginable scale.

The UN report on the State of World Population was published to coincide with the opening of the Habitat II conference in Istanbul. Representatives from the world's nations will be asked to act on the report's findings and steer development programmes towards urban education and health projects, especially for women, to improve the upward mobility of shanty-town dwellers. The UN Secretary-General, will also call for efforts to control the 'inevitable' march of the city. The UN is pushing for the development of a large number of manageable, medium-sized cities rather than a few, uncontrollable super-cities.

In 1950 the world had 83 cities with populations of 1,000,000 or more. Today there are 280. By 2015 there will be more than 500

Another UN agency, the International Labour Organisation (ILO) – is calling for redoubled efforts by wealthy countries and poor countries alike to create jobs for the urban poor. Otherwise, it warns, the armies of city dwellers living in poverty will exceed 1 billion by the end of the century.

'By 2000, one-half of humanity will be living and working in cities, with developing countries accounting for the major share of the world's new urban population,' said ILO deputy director, Katherine Hagen. 'These people will need jobs if the new cities are to develop as centres of economic opportunity and civilisation rather than zones of inequality and misery.'

The main report, by the UN Population Fund, stresses the potential benefits, as well as the menaces, presented by the urban explosion.

'The urban future carries many risks for the physical environment

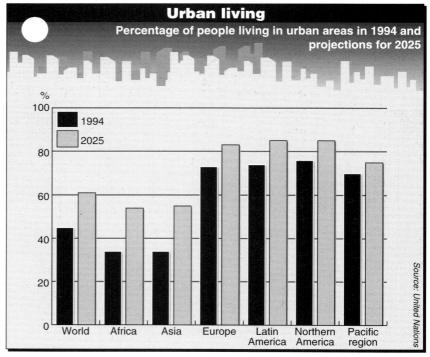

Urban living
Percentage of people living in urban areas in 1994 and projections for 2025

Source: United Nations

and natural resources, for social cohesion and for individual rights but it also offers vast opportunities. The experience of large cities as concentrations of human creativity and the highest forms of social organisation suggests that the future will open new avenues for human development.'

'Cities provide capital, labour and markets for entrepreneurs and innovators at all levels of economic activity. Cities already account for 60 to 80 per cent of the gross national product of many developing countries.'

Three factors explain the rapid growth of city populations, the report says. There is the migration into town of impoverished country-dwellers. There is a colonisation of outlying villages by urban conglomerations. But the largest factor is the population explosion among slum-dwelling citizens themselves. Despite the appallingly unhealthy conditions endured by people in the slums of places such as Lagos and Kinshasa, the urban birth-rate invariably outpaces the death-rate.

The report does point to hopeful signs in some Third World

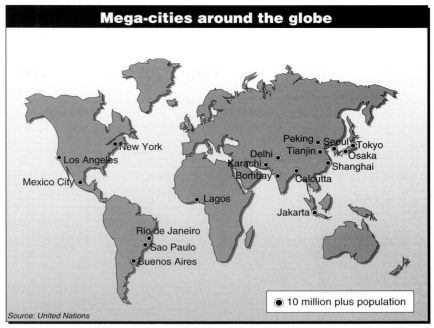

Mega-cities around the globe

New York
Los Angeles
Mexico City
Lagos
Rio de Janeiro
Sao Paulo
Buenos Aires
Peking
Seoul
Tokyo
Delhi
Tianjin
Osaka
Karachi
Shanghai
Bombay
Calcutta
Jakarta

● 10 million plus population

Source: United Nations

cities. One example is Bombay where progress has been made in replacing squatter homes with new dwellings.

At the other end of the scale, there are – especially in Africa – almost wholly dysfunctional cities, which have become nightmarish agglomerations of insanitary homes, ruined roads, abandoned services and crime.

'Increasing urbanisation has the potential for improving human life or increasing human misery,' the report says, 'Cities can . . . promote health or cause disease; empower people to realise their needs and desires or impose on them a simple struggle for basic survival. Which of these represents the urban future is a matter for us to decide.' © *The Independent May, 1997*

Sold down the river

The Thames is in crisis, not just because of its water loss. Daloni Carlisle reports on the steady destruction of the riverbank as developers tighten their hold

Kingston upon Thames. It's practically in the country. Along the river stretch described in the Department of Environment's new strategic Planning Guidance for the River Thames as being 'largely open in character', the bank is home to wildlife with swans dipping in and out of the water.

Except that a restaurant has just been built on the last of Kingston's alluvial beaches, destroying one of the few sites left where swans could get out of the water and the reed banks where bream and carp spawn and invertebrates breed.

Just up past John Lewis and the Bishop's pub, also built on alluvial beaches in the 1980s, a breeding site for kingfishers is threatened by plans for over 200 flats and a new theatre in a development that will rise eight floors from the river front. The developer, St George, has served eviction notices on the nine residential houseboats on the site.

'Alright, it's not a greenfield site,' says soon-to-be-homeless resident Gary Evans. 'But every night we have 15 to 20 swans nesting here and kingfishers. In the summer, when the reeds grow and the fish spawn, it

is an amazing sight. Where will they breed in future?'

Up and down the Thames, the story is the same. Bit by bit, the river is being put into a straitjacket and could soon become one long ribbon of prestigious office blocks and flats. One by one, the people who live and work on the Thames are being forced out. Boatyards are selling up or are unable to renew their leases as developers move in on valuable sites. The residential moorings are being replaced by resident-only pontoons for the owners of the new luxury flats. Meanwhile the foreshore where invertebrates breed and birds rest and feed is being replaced with vertical concrete and steel pilings.

Tough's Boatyard, established in 1887, at Teddington is a good example. It featured in the DoE's consultation document on its Thames strategy in June last year alongside the statement: 'Boat building, servicing and repair facilities are vital to the use of the river.' Developers have since levelled the yard. The first of three blocks of flats is nearing completion and 80 per cent are already sold at prices from £180,000 for a two-bedroom flat to over £650,000 for a penthouse suite. Boatyards with their slipways and peripheral wildlife sites are threatened at Richmond, Putney, Wandsworth, Chertsey and the Isle of Dogs.

'It's market forces,' shrugs the former owner, Mr Tough, as he wanders through the remains of the once-thriving concern. 'We are not getting the business any more.'

Where he shrugs, others are up in arms over the sterilisation of the Thames. Dido Berkeley has launched a High Court action against Fulham Football Club over its proposals to develop the site into flats and a new stadium. Backed by a consortium of architects and planners, she argues that the development will encroach on the Thames and destroy sloping banks so vital to wildlife along the Hammersmith-Fulham stretch of the river. Judgement is due in April.

'We're not against the football club,' she says. 'We just want a development that takes account of the community and the wider impact on the river.' London Wildlife Trust and the Campaign for the Protection of Rural England are both fighting to protect Thames-side wildlife habitats.

Mathew Frith, London Wildlife Trust conservation manager, says: 'There is no wild bank between Hammersmith and the Isle of Dogs. We are told that there are more fish in the Thames now than for 30 years and maybe that's true but everything else is going down the pan. Up and down the river authorities are engaging in cosmetic exercises to prettify the environment and getting rid of the rough areas that wildlife needs. Mud is essential.'

Environmental watchdogs have little faith in any of the regulatory authorities, and describe the strategic planning document with its commitments to the ecology of the Thames and mixed usage as 'flimsy'. James Cameron, a barrister and director of the Federation of International Environmental Law and Development (Field), says: 'Nobody has overall responsibility for the Thames and nobody looks on it from the ecological point of view. Unless you look at the whole picture you miss what's really happening to the river.'

Each piecemeal development that alters the flow of the river or the wildlife living along it will affect humans in unknown ways. And while the Government fails to enforce an EC directive requiring environmental impact assessments, no one will know what's going on, he says.

The Environment Agency is responsible for protecting the total river environment and has a formal policy objecting to destruction of the foreshore and encroachment onto the Thames – buildings that jut out into the river. The agency has objected to a number of developments and cites the MI6 building at Vauxhall as a good reason for its policy. 'Not only has it destroyed part of the foreshore but it has also caused localised scouring,' says spokeswoman Helen Hancock.

Its battle of the moment is the Greenwich bypass. 'The plan is to build a box along the foreshore through which cars would travel,' says Hancock. 'It would have tremendous effect right along the river. It would be the largest single encroachment on the Thames.'

The agency's approach is to work with planners, not against them and on March 26 it launched a best practice in river development policy. But anyone looking to the Environment Agency for real protection should perhaps look again. Approached to talk about the impact on the river of its substantial developments, Tony Carey, managing director of builders St George, says: 'We are aware of what the Environment Agency is saying and we agree with them. In the end they will support our project, there's no doubt about it. It [objecting] is their opening gambit and it's what we expect.'

Lady Berkeley is cynical too. 'Parks in London are protected as open spaces and that's what we need for the Thames. The Environment Agency cannot protect it because they have to put buildings first. The Thames is up for sale.'

© *The Guardian*
April, 1997

A new pride of place

Information from The Civic Trust

The British, unlike most other Europeans, do not seem to care much for their towns and cities. Time and again media comment focuses on the threat to the countryside but fails to stress the positive qualities and needs of urban areas. Yet they are where most people live and they are where the creativity to achieve a better quality of life for the nation has been concentrated in the past, and will need to be recreated in the future.

The Trust believes that there is now a need to think and act more positively about these centres of wealth, science, education, culture and energy. There is much within them to justify pride and even passion, not just the buildings and the spaces, but also the talents of their people and their communities. Yet that sense of pride is not always evident, in contrast to the feelings one can find in other European countries, and even as far away as Japan. In contrast also to the civic pride imparted in the past by philanthropic businessmen and municipal leaders such as Titus Salt in Bradford and Joseph Chamberlain in Birmingham.

The Trust wants to act both as a 'catalyst', stimulating creation of a greater sense of purpose and pride and also as an 'animateur' to help achieve a British 'Urban Renaissance'. We have termed this vision a new 'Pride of Place'. A pride felt by citizens about their street, neighbourhood, district, town and city. A pride born of involvement and a sense of belonging. It is not of course a new idea but it is one whose relevance is now very clear.

We have therefore drawn together a set of concerted actions and initiatives in two parts. The first part are linked themes, which underpin the drive for a new 'Pride of Place'. The second are specific suggestions for action drawn from the themes. Whilst the vision and themes should endure for some time, the action plan is focused on the next 2-3 years, and will be regularly revised.

In seeking to achieve a new 'Pride of Place', what vision do we seek to convey? It could not of course be a single end-state but we would expect it to have the following characteristics:-

- Community involvement across the whole spectrum of environmental decisions, with more direct community management.
- A significant reduction in the incidence of poverty and deprivation.
- Young people actively engaged in their communities and seeking to improve their surroundings.
- Local government with restored responsibility and finance for local action, working closely with its community and business partners.
- A broad pattern of sustainable regeneration which has resulted in new economic vitality, improved social cohesion, less environmental impact and a reduced demand on non-renewable resources.
- More people able and willing to live close to their work and associated facilities.
- Central and inner areas remodelled to provide a new mix of uses, with much more housing, catering for all social groups and with well-managed public spaces.
- Older buildings adapted more imaginatively to a varied range of new uses.
- New buildings which reflect well-understood principles of 'sustainable design' and 'urban design'.
- A transport system where use of the car and lorry is substantially reduced because attitudes have changed and investment in other transport has provided more choice.
- A vitality, diversity, and cultural richness in British towns and cities which are the envy of other countries.

• The above is an extract from *Pride of Place – The Civic Trust Manifesto*, published by the Civic Trust. See page 39 for address details.

© Civic Trust

All-green homes for people who promise not to buy a car

By John Arlidge, Scotland Correspondent

Designed by a Yorkshireman, built by Londoners, lived in by Scots – the homes of the future, where no one owns a car, trees replace tarmac, water is recycled and heating and lighting are free, are being built in Edinburgh.

Backed by Edinburgh Council and the Scottish Office, the £8 million estate is the most radical housing initiative since the sixties. Architects and planners say the environmentally friendly development will transform urban life.

A landscaped garden will surround more than 100 homes on the site of an old railway goods yard near the city centre. There are no roads, no parking spaces and no garages. Residents will sign an agreement not to own a car but to use one from a 'pool'.

Heating will be free all year round. Steam from factories will be used to heat homes and water, while solar panels on the roof of each home will provide lighting. Other energy-saving measures mean household bills will be up to 25 per cent below the UK average. Water from sinks and baths will be pumped into ponds, then filtered and purified in reed beds before being used for cleaning; conservatory-style windows will generate heat; rainwater will be collected to be used in bathrooms; and all household waste will be recycled.

The tenement-style estate, approved by councillors last week, is the 'greenest' in Britain. Alan Brown, director of Canmore Housing Association, which is behind the project, said: 'No one has tried the car-free design before and we are combining for the first time all the most advanced energy-saving technologies.'

The most radical element of the new scheme is the car ban. Residents will pay about £200 to join a council-run car club which will maintain and insure a fleet of vehicles in an on-site garage. They will be able to reserve cars at any time of the day or night at an hour's notice and will pay mileage and rental charges for each journey.

> '**There is now a substantial minority of people who will opt out of car ownership and in to a new way of life and transport**'

Although Britain's biggest developers have dismissed the car-free concept as unworkable, Canmore Housing Association has already received dozens of requests to reserve homes. Barry Cross, transport planning manager at Edinburgh Council, says that the response proves that the public is ready for pioneering 'pay-as-you-drive' schemes.

'As health worries grow, attitudes towards car use are changing,' he said. 'There is now a substantial minority of people who will opt out of car ownership and in to a new way of life and transport.'

Bryan Thomas, the architect from Yorkshire who designed the estate, agrees. 'The British traditionally love their cars and view anyone who does not have one as some sort of sexual deviant. But times are moving on.'

Other bold visions from planners and architects have been laid waste by chronic mismanagement, lax building standards and opposition from local people. Those behind the Edinburgh project, who are negotiating with London contractors to carry out the work, insist they have learnt the lessons of the past.

Mr Brown says the ideas behind the new scheme will transform inner-city life. 'House builders are too conservative and out of touch. They have not realised what ordinary people already know – that car ownership and city living are incompatible and that we can live in a more ecologically sound way. When this project takes off, the ambience and style of life will change and others will want to follow.'

He may be right. Later this year Camden Council in London will vote on whether to copy Edinburgh's example. Other local authorities are discussing projects. For many city dwellers, freedom is the end of the road.

British wake up to cities that never sleep

Sleepless in Sheffield? The city is about to host a conference on how best to deal with 24-hour urban life as society continues to move from the suburbs and to rediscover the joys of street life, writes Tom Leonard

The queue outside Quatre-Vingt usually begins to clear by about 4am on a Sunday morning.

For most it has been a hard night's clubbing, for others a pre-work coffee, that brings them to the 24-hour, seven-day-a-week, café bar in Chelsea.

Inside, the walls are painted bright colours, the chairs are hard, and the hands of the wall clock move frenetically.

'It's done for a reason,' explains Simon Prideaux, the duty manager. 'We want to make it homely but not so comfortable that people fall asleep.'

Mr Prideaux is not the only one who doesn't want people to nod off too early. Later this week, planners, architects, council leaders, magistrates and senior police officers will congregate in Sheffield for a two-day conference devoted to the ideal of the city that never sleeps.

If we had more people like Quatre-Vingt's clientele, the thinking goes, our cities would become more vibrant and safer.

Now in its fourth year, the National Conference on the 24-Hour City has moved on from debating the merits of longer licensing hours to embrace the overall future of life in our cities.

The eminence of the speakers and delegates to this year's conference supports organisers' claims that the theme is now being taken seriously by the decision-makers. Among those addressing this week's conference are Richard Wells, chief constable of South Yorkshire, Bill Morris, general secretary of the Transport and General Workers' Union, and Keith Vaz, shadow minister of environment and regeneration.

Delegates will be repeating their argument that the exodus from the inner cities that began in most of Britain after the Second World War is now in reverse. Many people, particularly the young, want to live right in the middle of the city.

Unfortunately they are also discovering that nightlife in Britain's run-down, dangerous inner cities is much less exciting than that in the streets of other European cities such as Barcelona, Amsterdam and Berlin.

> *For most it has been a hard night's clubbing, for others a pre-work coffee, that brings them to the 24-hour, seven-day-a-week, café bar in Chelsea*

While our cities are still keeping office hours, the rest of society is increasingly not. International communications and the trend towards self-employment mean that the nine-to-five ritual is no longer the norm. 'Time-shifting is the developing fashion,' says Dr John Montgomery, a lecturer in planning at the University of Reading and one of the conference's original founders.

Television and shopping are available virtually 24-hours-a-day but the city at night is still seen as a problem that has to be regulated, with early closing times sending people home to bed at a respectable hour. Dr Montgomery and his associates want not only to keep the cities open for longer but to make them bring people together.

Help will be coming from abroad with talks by urban designers from Barcelona and Copenhagen. Sceptics who doubt the British climate's ability to accommodate Mediterranean-style café culture can go and listen to Hafdis Haflidarsdottir, an architect at Reykjavik City Council, explain how Iceland copes in making its capital hum all year round.

One pressing issue this week will be making night-time city centres more attractive to older generations. The big brewery groups, for instance, will be encouraged to moderate their current tendency to cater almost exclusively for the 18-25-year-old market and instead convert some of their city-centre pubs into Continental-style café bars.

'The only way we're going to civilise the lager lout culture is to have grown-up people around,' says Dr Montgomery. He cites the example of a small square in The Lanes in Brighton where the opening of a café bar, and the older customers it attracted, drastically cut trouble from younger drinkers in a pub nearby.

Conference delegates will also be swapping news about the '24-hour zones' that have already sprung up with council support, in previously run-down, commercial areas in cities such as Sheffield, Leeds and Manchester.

Dr Montgomery believes that whatever their size, cities will benefit economically through extra revenue and increased employment.

Meanwhile, the Quatre-Vingt's laid-back antidote to west London's frenetic world of pubs and nightclubs offers the very kind of civilised 24-hour city life which the conference delegates seem to be seeking to create.

INDEX

ADDITIONAL RESOURCES

The Civic Trust
17 Carlton House Terrace
London, SW1Y 5AW
Tel: 0171 930 0914
Fax: 0171 321 0180
Works to improve the quality of
life by creating, enhancing and
sustaining a built environment of
quality, social well-being and
economic health in partnership
with the community, government
and business. Publishes *Pride of
Place* and a quarterly newsletter
Urban Focus.

Commission for the New Towns
Central Business Exchange
414-428 Midsummer Boulevard
Central Milton Keynes, MK9 2EA
Tel: 01908 696300
Fax: 01908 691333
A Government-backed property
agency charged with the disposal of
land and premises in the English
New Towns.

**Council for the Protection of
Rural England (CPRE)**
Warwick House
25 Buckingham Palace Road
London, SW1W 0PP
Tel: 0171 976 6433
Fax: 0171 976 6373
Keeps readers abreast of current
issues and promotes positive
solutions. Publishes *CPRE Voice*.
Produces publications.

Countryside Commission
John Dower House
Crescent Place
Cheltenham, GL50 3RA
Tel: 01242 521381
Fax: 01242 584270
Protects and enhances the
countryside for the general public.
Produces publications including
Public Attitudes to the Countryside.

EarthKind
Bounds Green Road
London, N22 4EU
Tel: 0181 889 1595
Fax: 0181 881 7662
Produces publications including
their magazine *The Living World*.

Forum for the Future
Thornbury House
18 High Street
Cheltenham, GL50 1DZ
Tel: 01242 262729
Aims to work in partnership with
and guide decision-makers in
industry and government to build a
sustainable way of life. Publishes
Green Futures, a magazine seeking
to spread the message and practice
of sustainable development.

Friends of the Earth
26-28 Underwood Street
London, N1 7JQ
Tel: 0171 490 1555
Fax: 0171 490 0881
As an independent environmental
group, Friends of the Earth produce
a comprehensive range of leaflets,
books and in-depth briefings and
reports.

House Builders' Federation
82 New Cavendish Street
London, W1M 8AD
Tel: 0171 580 5588
Fax: 0171 323 1697
Produces *Home* magazine.

**National Housing and Town
Planning Council**
14-18 Old Street
London, EC1V 9AB
Tel: 0171 251 2363
Fax: 0171 608 2830
Works to achieve better standards
and conditions in housing, to
promote better town planning and
to help to improve the natural and
built environments. Produces
publications.

Open Spaces Society
25a Bell Street
Henley-on-Thames
Oxon, RG9 2BA
Tel: 01491 573535
Works to preserve commons, public
open spaces and greens for public
use in both town and country;
protects existing public paths for
walkers, horseriders and cyclists.
Produces various publications
including a magazine, *Open Space*.

**Royal Town Planning Institute
(RTPI)**
26 Portland Place
London, W1N 4BE
Tel: 0171 636 9107
Fax: 0171 232 1582
Advances the science of town
planning in all its aspects for the
benefit of the public and the
environment.

Rural Action National Team
Freepost GL485
Cirencester, GL7 1BR
Tel: 01285 659599
Fax: 01285 654537
A partnership of organisations
working for a better environment.
It has a national office, but grants
and advice are administered
locally.

**The SAFE Alliance
(Sustainable Agriculture, Food
& Environment)**
38 Ebury Street
London, SW1W 0LU
Tel: 0171 823 5660
Fax: 0171 823 5673
The alliance has established itself
as a major voice in the debate on
agriculture and food policy, and
works with a network of similar
alliances across Europe.

The Wildlife Trust
The Green
Witcham Park
Waterside South
Lincoln, LN5 7JR
Tel: 01522 544400
Fax: 01522 511616
Has a nationwide network of local
trusts working to protect wildlife in
town and country.

**Town and Country Planning
Association**
17 Carlton House Terrace
London, SW1Y 5AS
Tel: 0171 930 8903
Fax: 0171 930 3280
Provides an informed and
independent voice on national,
regional and environmental
planning. Produces publications.

ACKNOWLEDGEMENTS

The publisher is grateful for permission to reproduce the following material.

While every care has been taken to trace and acknowledge copyright, the publisher tenders its apology for any accidental infringement or where copyright has proved untraceable. The publisher would be pleased to come to a suitable arrangement in any such case with the rightful owner.

Chapter One: Countryside under threat?

Love affair with the countryside, © Countryside Commission, January/February 1996, *Current vs. preferred place of residence*, © Countryside Commission, *Royal Commission adds to fears over Britain's vanishing fields*, © Telegraph Group Limited, London 1996, *City exodus threat to rural areas*, © The Guardian, March 1997, *Awareness of change in the countryside*, © Countryside Commission, *British still seek a rural idyll, and ruin it*, © The Observer, May 1996, *Development and economics*, © Countryside Commission, *Townies 'to blame for crisis in the country'*, © The Daily Mail, February 1997, *£1m shopping offer that divides a town*, © The Daily Mail, January 1997, *Councils 'ignore guideline on out-of-town shopping'*, © Telegraph Group Limited, London 1997, *How to campaign on supermarket developments*, © S.A.F.E., *Responding to planning applications*, © Council for the Protection of Rural England (CPRE), Autumn 1996, *Save our shops with car tax on malls, say MPs*, © The Daily Mail, March 1997, *New homes best sited in towns, says Minister*, © Telegraph Group Limited, London 1996, *Growth in number of households 1991-2016*, © HMSO Reproduced with the kind permission of Her Majesty's Stationery Office, *Ghastly sign of the times*, © Telegraph Group Limited, London 1996, *Beating a rural retreat in the age of the City Kitty*, © The Daily Mail, January 1997, © *Plan for doubling the size of English Woodlands*, © The Guardian, October 1996, *Woodland creation*, © Forestry Authority, *Tranquillity*, © Countryside Commission, January/February 1996, *Living spaces*, © The Open Spaces Society, *People abandon cities for the country life*, © The Guardian, December 1996, *Household growth*, © House Builders' Federation, January 1997, *Towns to grow in green fields*, © The Independent, August 1996, *Why village England wants to be kept in dark*, © Telegraph Group Limited, London 1996.

Chapter Two: Urban life

Urban footprints, © Council for the Protection of Rural England (CPRE), *Why I should be stopped from fleeing to suburbia*, © The Independent, November 1996, *Urban development*, © Commission for the New Towns, *London's calling*, © Green Futures Publications, April/May 1997, *Super-cities threaten to swallow humanity*, © The Independent, May 1996, *Sold down the river*, © The Guardian, April 1997, *A new pride of place*, © Civic Trust, 1996, *All-green homes for people who promise not to buy a car*, © The Observer, April 1997, *British wake up to cities that never sleep*, © Telegraph Group Limited, London 1996.

Photographs and Illustrations

Pages 1, 4, 20: Michaela Bloomfield, pages 3, 7, 11, 15, 22, 27: Ken Pyne, pages 8, 24, 28: Andrew Smith, page 34: Katherine Fleming.

Craig Donnellan
Cambridge
September, 1997